THE INFOGRAPHIC BOOK OF CYCLING

VELOPEDIA

THE INFOGRAPHIC BOOK OF CYCLING
VELOPEDIA
ROBERT DINEEN

Aurum
Press

Contents

The evolution of the racing bike

Squint a little and there appears to be little obvious difference between Michaux's mid-19th century leg-driven Velocipede and Chris Froome's pedal-powered Pinarello on which he won the 2016 Tour de France. But every part of the bike has changed, with materials evolving to offer ever lighter, more aerodynamic and faster machines.

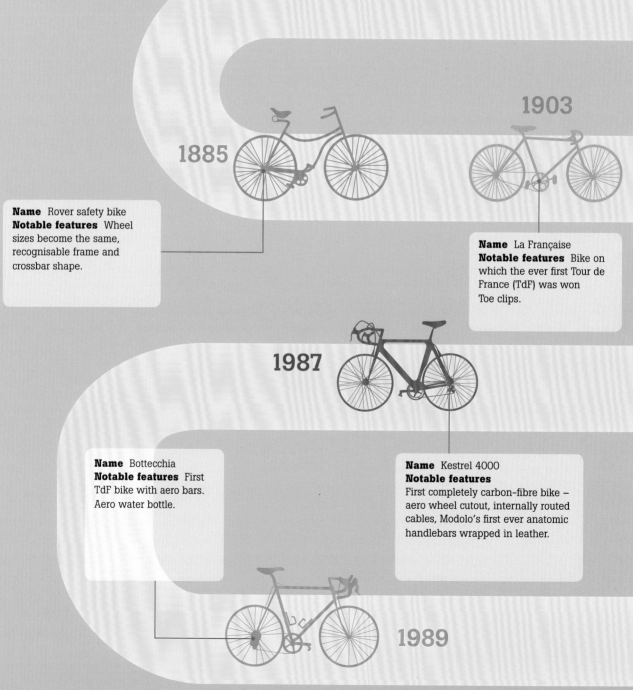

1903

1885

Name Rover safety bike
Notable features Wheel sizes become the same, recognisable frame and crossbar shape.

Name La Française
Notable features Bike on which the ever first Tour de France (TdF) was won Toe clips.

1987

Name Bottecchia
Notable features First TdF bike with aero bars. Aero water bottle.

Name Kestrel 4000
Notable features
First completely carbon-fibre bike – aero wheel cutout, internally routed cables, Modolo's first ever anatomic handlebars wrapped in leather.

1989

1878

Name Penny farthing
Notable features Radical difference in wheel sizes.

1868

Name Michaux velocipede
Notable features Earliest bike used in a race — James Moore won the first cycling race on this.

1937

Name Mercier Hutchinson
Notable features First year in which derailleur (shifting-chain gear) was legalised.

1972

Name Alan
Notable features First aluminium frame.

Name Lotus 110
Notable features Formula One motor racing engineering practice applied to a bicycle. Sleek aerodynamic shape.

Name Pinarello Dogma F8
Notable features ONDA F8 fork, example of precision aerodynamic craftsmanship.

2015

1996

Tour de France by numbers

The history of the world's greatest bike race has thrown up some startling figures. Here is a selection of the most important*.

2,242 km

3,519km
Distance of first Tour in 1903, which comprised six stages.
Distance of 2016 Tour, which had 21 stages.

103
Editions of the race, including 2016.

24.046
kilometre/hour
Firmin Lambot's average speed when the Belgian won the slowest ever Tour in 1919.

41.654
kilometre/hour
Lance Armstrong's speed when he won the fastest ever Tour de France in 2005 (which he was subsequently stripped of).

50.4
kilometre/hour
Mario Cipollini's speed when he won the fastest ever massed-start stage from Laval to Blois (194.5km) in 1999.

8
Most stage wins in a single Tour, a record shared by **Merckx** (1970, 1974), the Frenchman **Charles Pélissier** (1930) and Belgium's **Freddy Maertens** (1976).

10
Years is the longest gap between Tour victories. Gino Bartali (Ita) won in 1938 and 1948.

5
Five riders share the record of five victories
Maurice Garin (Fra)
Jacques Anquetil (Fra)
Eddy Merckx (Bel)
Bernard Hinault (Fra)
Miguel Indurain (Spa)

19
Age of youngest ever Tour winner, Henri Cornet (Fra), in 1904.

36
Age of oldest ever Tour winner, Firmin Lambot (Bel), in 1922.

36
French victories, the most for any nation. Belgium is second with 18 and Spain third on 13.

34
Eddy Merckx's record number of stage victories.

6
Most green-jersey victories, held by Erik Zabel (Ger), 1996-2001.

3
Most white-jersey victories, shared by Jan Ullrich (Ger) 1996-98 and Andy Schleck (Lux) 2008-10.

7
Most polka-dot jersey victories, held by Richard Virenque (Fra), 1994-97, 1999, 2003-04.

12,000 francs
Prize-fee for the first Tour. This was worth six times what most factory workers in France then would have earnt in a year.

450,000 euros
First prize for 2016 Tour. This was 12 times the annual national salary in France.

4
Riders have died competing in the race, **Adolphe Helière** (1910), **Francisco Cepeda** (1935), **Tom Simpson** (1967) and **Fabio Casartelli** (1995). Helière drowned while swimming on the rest day.

7
Fatal accidents to victims other than riders.

8 seconds
Smallest winning margin, the time-difference by which Greg LeMond (US), *left*, defeated Laurent Fignon (Fra), *right*, in 1989.

17
The record number of appearances on the Tour, shared by **George Hincapie** (US), **Stuart O'Grady** (Aus) and **Jens Voight** (Ger).

2hr 49min 45sec
Biggest winning margin, by which Maurice Garin (Fra) beat Lucie (Fra) in 1903.

20
Hinault's record number of time-trial victories.

*Figures correct up to 2016

Power game

Cyclists' training methods have been transformed since it became possible to measure accurately how much power they generate in the saddle. The technology was first made available in the 1990s, though its potential was only fully unlocked in the following decade as the most innovative teams, such as the British national side, constructed their training regimes around the data produced by power meters. The data is useful because it is the best objective measure of exactly how hard a rider can work.

HOW MANY PROFESSIONAL CYCLISTS WOULD IT TAKE TO CHARGE A...?*

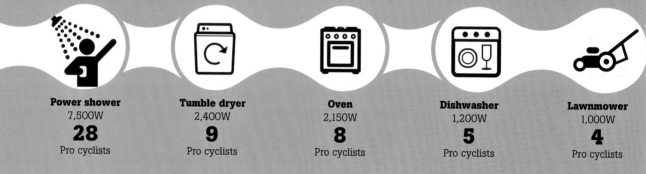

Power shower	Tumble dryer	Oven	Dishwasher	Lawnmower
7,500W	2,400W	2,150W	1,200W	1,000W
28	**9**	**8**	**5**	**4**
Pro cyclists	Pro cyclists	Pro cyclists	Pro cyclists	Pro cyclists

MEASURING DEVICES

There are several ways of measuring power output on a bike, including sensors in the chain and on the roller of a stationary home trainer, but the most efficient and most popular is the sensor placed on the crankset, which measures power through the pressure placed on the chainring and translates it to wattage. It was developed by the German engineering company Schoberer Rad Messtechnik and has become commonplace in the peloton.

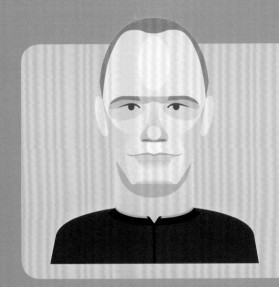

FROOME'S BIG REVEAL

Perhaps the most studied set of rider data was released in 2015 when Team Sky agreed to publish the results of physical tests that Chris Froome underwent to allay accusations that his performance in winning that year's Tour de France was too good to be true and therefore the result of doping. It showed that his peak power was 525W and he could sustain 419W over 20-40 minutes. This was no better than similar tests he did in 2007, suggesting he was riding clean. The critical difference was that he was 6kg lighter which, according to one scientist, meant he was operating at 'the upper limit of human performance'.

*Based on the amount of power a rider produces on a mountain stage of a Grand Tour. Appliance figures are all minimum wattage.

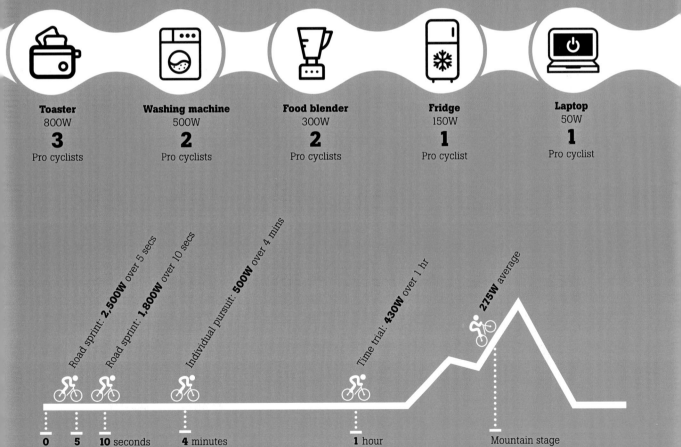

Toaster 800W	**Washing machine** 500W	**Food blender** 300W	**Fridge** 150W	**Laptop** 50W
3	**2**	**2**	**1**	**1**
Pro cyclists	Pro cyclists	Pro cyclists	Pro cyclist	Pro cyclist

Road sprint: **2,500W** over 5 secs

Road sprint: **1,800W** over 10 secs

Individual pursuit: **500W** over 4 mins

Time trial: **430W** over 1 hr

275W average

| 0 | 5 | 10 seconds | 4 minutes | 1 hour | Mountain stage of a Grand Tour |

ELITE FIGURES
Typical power outputs in professional races

The Hour Record

The record for distance covered without being paced in an hour is the most prestigious record in cycling. Timed on a track and from a stationary start, it has attracted some of the biggest names in the sport and undergone several incarnations as the UCI has adjusted the rules to keep up with developments in technology.

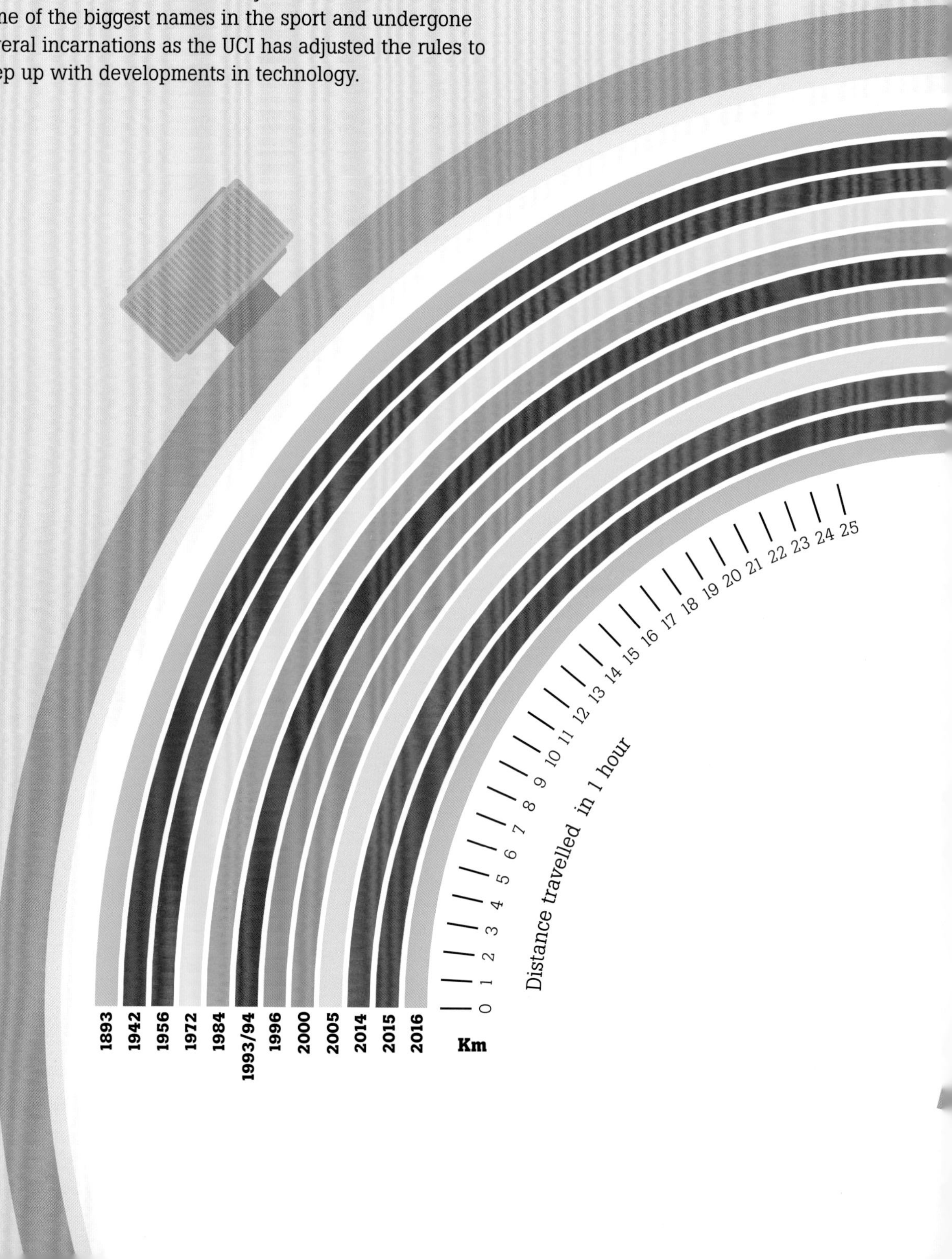

Distance travelled in 1 hour

0 1 2 3 4 5 6 7 8 9 10 11 12 13 14 15 16 17 18 19 20 21 22 23 24 25

1893
1942
1956
1972
1984
1993/94
1996
2000
2005
2014
2015
2016

Km

The UCI created
two categories for the
hour record in 1997 in response
to advances in technology. One was
the UCI Hour Record, which restricted
competitors to roughly the same
equipment as Eddy Merckx, banning time-
trial helmets, disc or tri-spoke wheels,
aerodynamic bars and monocoque
frames. The other was the Best Human
Effort (BHE), in which modern
equipment was permitted.

2014
The UCI
unified the two
categories, restricting
all bikes to the
specifications of a
standard track bike.

35.325km

45.798km

46.159km

49.431km

50.808km

51.596km and 52.713km

56.375km

49.441km

49.700km

51.110km

47.980km (WOMEN'S RECORD)

54.526km

35 36 37 38 39 40 41 42 43 44 45 46 47 48 49 50 51 52 53 54 55 56 57 58 59 60

Distance travelled in 1 hour

Km

Evelyn Stevens
Sir Bradley Wiggins
Jens Voigt
Ondrej Sosenka
Chris Boardman
Chris Boardman
Graeme Obree
Francesco Moser
Eddy Merckx
Jacques Anquetil
Fausto Coppi
Henri Desgrange

Key

▲ Restricted bike specification

● Unrestricted bike specification

■ Standard track bike

15

The World Tour teams

Eighteen teams contested the 28 events that made up the World Tour schedule in 2016, with lower-ranked teams invited to compete on a race-by-race basis. Overall, Movistar have been the most successful team of late, being ranked first each season from 2013 to 2015.

AG2R La Mondiale
Country of origin:
France
General manager:
Vincent Lavenu
Directeur sportif:
Laurent Biondi
Principal rider:
Jean-Christophe Péraud

Astana Pro Team
Country of origin:
Kazakhstan
General manager:
Alexandr Vinokourov
Directeur sportif:
Dmitriy Fofonov
Principal rider:
Vincenzo Nibali

BMC Racing Team
Country of origin: USA
General manager:
James L Ochowicz
Directeur sportif:
Allan Peiper
Principal rider:
Tejay van Garderen

Cannondale-Drapac (Pro Team)
Country of origin: USA
General manager:
Jonathan Vaughters
Directeur sportif:
Charles Wegelius
Principal riders:
Pierre Rolland and
Andrew Talansky

Etixx-Quick-Step
Country of origin:
Belgium
General manager:
Patrick Lefevere
Directeur sportif:
Wilfried Peeters
Principal rider:
Tony Martin

FDJ
Country of origin:
France
General manager:
Marc Madiot
Directeur sportif:
Yvon Madiot
Principal rider:
Thibaut Pinot

IAM Cycling
Country of origin:
Switzerland
General manager:
Michel Thétaz
Directeur sportif:
Rik Verbrugghe
Principal rider:
Mathias Frank

Lampre-Merida
Country of origin: Italy
General manager:
Brent Copeland
Directeur sportif:
Philippe Mauduit
Principal rider:
Rui Costa

Lotto Soudal
Country of origin:
Belgium
General manager:
Marc Sergeant
Directeur sportif:
Mario Aerts
Principal rider:
Andre Greipel

Movistar Team
Country of origin: Spain
General manager:
Eusebio Unzué Labiano
Directeur sportif:
Eusebio Unzué Labiano
Principal rider:
Nairo Quintana

ORICA-Bike Exchange
Country of origin:
Australia
General manager:
Shayne Bannan
Directeur sportif:
Matthew White
Principal rider:
Michael Matthews

Team Dimension Data
Country of origin: South
Africa
General manager:
Douglas Ryder
Directeur sportif:
Jens Zemke
Principal rider:
Edvald Boasson Hagen

Team Giant-Alpecin
Country of origin:
Germany
General manager:
Iwan Spekenbrink
Directeur sportif:
Rudi Kemna
Principal rider:
John Degenkolb

Team Katusha
Country of origin:
Russia
General manager:
Viatcheslav Ekimov
Directeur sportif:
Jose Azevedo
Principal rider:
Joaquim Rodríguez

Team Lotto NL-Jumbo
Country of origin:
Netherlands
General manager:
Richard Plugge
Directeur sportif:
Nico Verhoeven
Principal riders:
Wilco Kelderman and
Robert Gesink

Team Sky
Country of origin:
Great Britain
General manager:
David Brailsford
Directeur sportif:
Nicolas Portal
Principal rider:
Chris Froome

Tinkoff
Country of origin:
Russia
General manager:
Stefano Feltrin
Directeur sportif:
Steven De Jongh
Principal rider:
Alberto Contador

Trek-Segafredo
Country of origin: USA
General manager:
Luca Guercilena
Directeur sportif:
Alain Gallopin
Principal rider:
Bauke Mollema

Greatest rivalries

Elite bike racing is never more exciting than when it is illuminated by a personal rivalry. Here are some of the most compelling.

Anquetil

Poulidor

> **'Sorry, Raymond, you're going to finish second again.'**
> Anquetil on his deathbed, 1987

JACQUES ANQUETIL v RAYMOND POULIDOR
France   *France*

Roots Anquetil invariably beat Poulidor in stage races but hated that his rival was more popular with the French public, who connected with Poulidor's more emotional character and with his struggles against Anquetil at a time when life was hard for the common man.

Standout duel Poulidor came closest to winning the 1964 Tour when he beat his rival in an epic battle up the *Puy-de-Dôme* on the final mountain stage, only for Anquetil then to claim overall victory on the final-day time trial.

ALFREDO BINDA
Italy
v
LEARCO GUERRA
Italy

Roots Guerra had public and State support, as he aligned himself with Italy's ruling fascists, and was open and humble. Binda was apolitical and regarded as cold and calculating, alienating him from fans.

Standout duel At the 1933 Giro d'Italia, Guerra suffered a bad crash after his bike touched Binda's. The former was taken to hospital and forced out of the race, which Binda went on to win.

What they said 'Whilst Binda was all smooth, effortless class, Guerra was a throwback to bygone days, a cycling warrior and unwitting mascot for Il Duce'
• *Herbie Skyes, cycling author.*

GINO BARTALI
Italy
v
FAUSTO COPPI
Italy

Roots These compatriots polarised Italian fans. Being older, conservative and deeply religious, Bartali appealed to the older generation, while Coppi was younger, secular, innovative and the hero of the younger public.

Standout duel At the 1948 World Road Race, the tension between them was such that both men dismounted their bikes and retired from the race rather than help the other one as team-mates on the Italian national team.

What they said 'In Italy, you learn in school about their rivalry and people still debate which one was better. They still have that conversation at dinner'
• *Marco Pinotti (Italy), former professional.*

'Journalists in France think everything Bernard has done has been to help me. It's been the contrary. It's been to try to win the race himself.'

LeMond, after his triumph at the 1986 Tour

FRANCESCO MOSER
Italy
V
GIUSEPPE SARONNI
Italy

Roots Ultimately, the rivalry was down to both men having to battle for affection from the Italian public, though it was fuelled by them disliking each other and being very different characters, with Moser the extrovert risk-taker, while Saronni was quiet and cunning.

Standout duel At the 1981 Tirreno-Adriatico, Saronni tracked a Moser break and attacked at the last moment to win, before declaring: 'Moser? I can beat him in tennis shoes.'

What they said 'Ours was a true rivalry, sincere, authentic, not artificial. We were too different in origin, character, style. We were not able to become friends, even when we retired'
• *Moser, 2015.*

STEPHEN ROCHE
Ireland
V
ROBERTO VISENTINI
Italy

Roots In 1987, Roche and Visentini were declared co-leaders of the Carrera-Inoxpran team going into the Giro d'Italia, the Giro and the World Road Race.

Standout duel On the 15th stage, with Visentini wearing the maglia rosa, Roche defied team orders by attacking Visentini. The move, which led to Roche's own team-mates chasing him down, earned the Irishman a lead that he never relinquished – despite constant abuse from Italian fans.

What they said 'Being attacked by opponents was normal, but it was my team-mate and I could just not stomach it. Roche's attack was unacceptable'
• *Visentini, 2014.*

BERNARD HINAULT V GREG LEMOND
France   *USA*

Roots In 1986, with both riding for the La Vie Claire team, Hinault had promised to help LeMond win the Tour because the American had done likewise for the Frenchman a year earlier.

Standout duel The entire 1986 Tour, during which Hinault repeatedly attacked LeMond. Hinault initially claimed he was trying to whittle out LeMond's rivals, but after LeMond had let him win the Alpe d'Huez stage, then said he wanted the title. The American still went on to win the Tour, though.

The nearly-men of the Tour

Finishing on the podium at the Tour de France without actually winning it can be a bittersweet achievement – a limited reward for superhuman effort. These riders have managed it the most often of all.

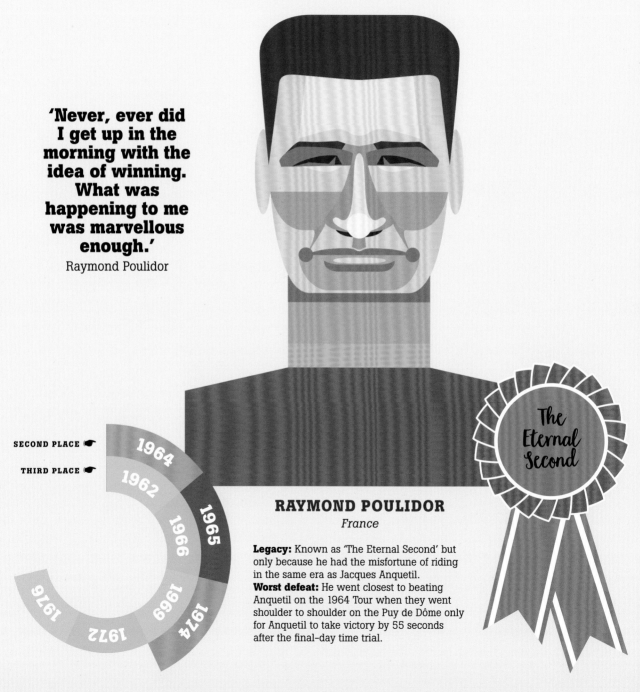

'Never, ever did I get up in the morning with the idea of winning. What was happening to me was marvellous enough.'
Raymond Poulidor

SECOND PLACE ☞

THIRD PLACE ☞

1964
1962
1965
1966
1969
1974
1972
1976

The Eternal Second

RAYMOND POULIDOR
France

Legacy: Known as 'The Eternal Second' but only because he had the misfortune of riding in the same era as Jacques Anquetil.
Worst defeat: He went closest to beating Anquetil on the 1964 Tour when they went shoulder to shoulder on the Puy de Dôme only for Anquetil to take victory by 55 seconds after the final-day time trial.

SECOND PLACE ☞

THIRD PLACE ☞

GUSTAVE GARRIGOU
France

Legacy: One of the greatest ever competitors, finishing in the top ten in 96 of the 117 stages he tackled.

Worst defeat: He was favourite for the 1912 Tour as the leader of a French team only for them to take on the Belgian Odile DeFraye at the last minute to generate publicity. DeFraye outsprinted Garrigou on stages two and three, which proved crucial to the latter being denied overall victory.

SECOND PLACE ☞

THIRD PLACE ☞

LUCIEN VAN IMPE
Belgium

Legacy: Van Impe won the King of the Mountains jersey six times but even that has a twist. He claimed he refrained from winning it a seventh time because he did not want to trump his mentor, Federico Bahamontes (Spa).

Worst defeat: Van Impe actually won the Tour in 1976 though is remembered just as much for his defeats. None was more difficult than the 1981 Tour when Bernard Hinault (Fra) dominated the race, leading from stage six until the end.

SECOND PLACE ☞

JOOP ZOETEMELK
Netherlands

Legacy: An unfair joke said that Zoetemelk never acquired a tan on the Tour because he always rode in Eddy Merckx's shadow.

Worst defeat: In 1976, with Merckx injured, a grave tactical error cost Zoetemelk victory on the Tour when he failed to give chase to eventual winner Lucien Van Impe on the 14th stage.

SECOND PLACE ☞

THIRD PLACE ☞

JAN ULLRICH
Germany

Legacy: For years, Ullrich was popular as the man who pushed Lance Armstrong closest, but his credit was lost when the German admitted in retirement to blood doping.

Worst defeat: Ullrich said his third consecutive runners-up spot in 2000 led him to fall into depression the following year.

The calendar decoded

Over the past few years, the UCI has been busy trying to streamline the professional cycling calendar to make it more understandable to fans, but the truth is that even devotees of the sport can struggle to work out its ranking system for teams and races.

World Tour

Code: WT

Grand Tours*

Monuments

World Championships

*Rulers at war** In a bitter row with the UCI over reform of the sport, the influential ASOS organisation said in December 2015 that it would withdraw its races from the World Tour calendar for 2017. ASOS owns the Tour de France, Paris-Nice and Paris-Roubaix among others though it was not clear if it meant all of its races would be involved in the boycott.

Tour of Turkey

Hors Categorie

Code: 1. HC (one-day races)
       2. HC (stage races)

Paris-Tours

Kuurne-Brussels-Kuurne

Tour of Utah

THE RACES

Categorie One

Code: 1.1 (one-day races)
       2.1 (stage races)

Le Samyn (Belgium)

Tour of Yorkshire

Categorie Two

Code: 1.2 (one-day races)
       2.2 (stage races)

Tour de Normandie

Paris-Troyes

THE HARD CLIMB

Quite how the UCI classifies races is unclear and the decision-making process has upset more than a few organisers because the higher-category races attract bigger prize funds, more UCI points and therefore better riders. When the Tour of Britain was denied a promotion, its organisers went on record to 'register their disappointment at the continued lack of communication from the UCI'.

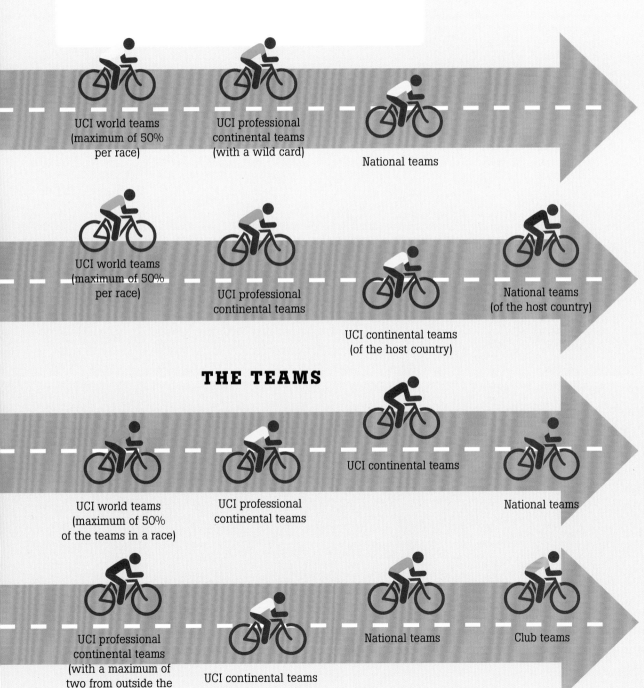

UCI world teams (maximum of 50% per race)

UCI professional continental teams (with a wild card)

National teams

UCI world teams (maximum of 50% per race)

UCI professional continental teams

UCI continental teams (of the host country)

National teams (of the host country)

THE TEAMS

UCI world teams (maximum of 50% of the teams in a race)

UCI professional continental teams

UCI continental teams

National teams

UCI professional continental teams (with a maximum of two from outside the host country)

UCI continental teams

National teams

Club teams

ICON Fausto Coppi

To the countless Italian fans who revered him, Fausto Coppi was *Il Campionissimo*, the champion of champions, whose talent and charisma ushered in a golden era for cycling and ensured him iconic status in its history. With seven Grand Tour victories and a clutch of other titles to his name, Coppi's palmares easily stands up alongside the best and he surely would have won more races had the Second World War not interrupted his career in its prime. Coppi, however, is remembered also for his life away from the saddle, especially the extramarital affair that divided his conservative Italian society. Combined with his sad death from malaria aged only 40, it made him the sport's greatest romantic hero.

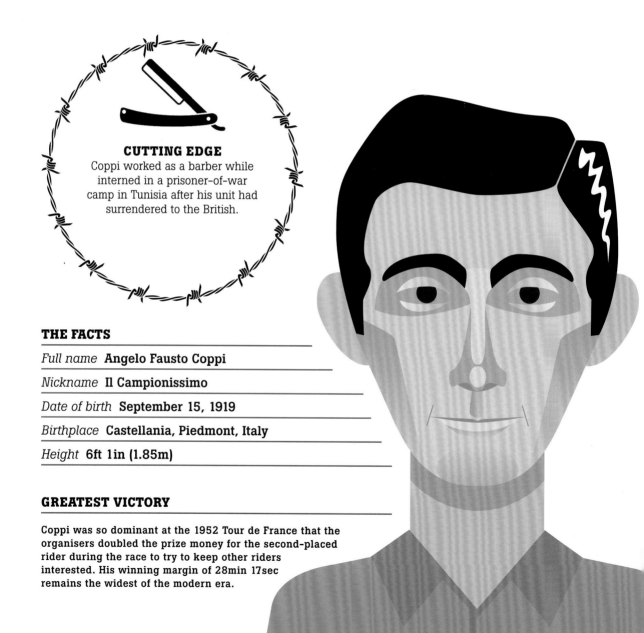

CUTTING EDGE

Coppi worked as a barber while interned in a prisoner-of-war camp in Tunisia after his unit had surrendered to the British.

THE FACTS

Full name **Angelo Fausto Coppi**

Nickname **Il Campionissimo**

Date of birth **September 15, 1919**

Birthplace **Castellania, Piedmont, Italy**

Height **6ft 1in (1.85m)**

GREATEST VICTORY

Coppi was so dominant at the 1952 Tour de France that the organisers doubled the prize money for the second-placed rider during the race to try to keep other riders interested. His winning margin of 28min 17sec remains the widest of the modern era.

THE MAJOR VICTORIES

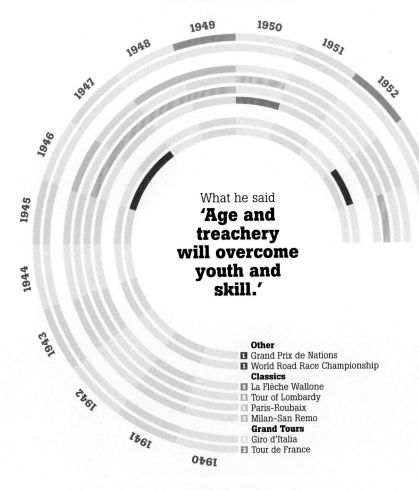

1948 1949 1950 1951
1947   1952
1946   1953
1945   1954
1944
1943
1942
1941
1940

What he said
'Age and treachery will overcome youth and skill.'

Other
1 Grand Prix de Nations
1 World Road Race Championship
Classics
5 La Flèche Wallone
5 Tour of Lombardy
1 Paris-Roubaix
3 Milan-San Remo
Grand Tours
5 Giro d'Italia
2 Tour de France

THE TEAMS

1938–39
Dopolavoro Tortona

1939–1942
Legnano

1945
Cicli Nulli Roma

1945–55
Bianchi

1956–57
Carpano-Coppi

1958
Bianchi-Pirelli

1959
Tricofilina-Coppi

Coppi had signed a contract for 1960 to ride for the San Pellegrino team but died before the start of the season.

'The vein! The vein!'
His great rival Gino Bartali would ask a team-mate to ride behind Coppi and loudly identify a chronic swelling behind Coppi's right knee that emerged under stress.

PAPAL PROBLEM
Coppi scandalised Italy when he left his wife for Giulia Occhini, who was also married, prompting Pope Pius XIII to plead with Coppi to give up the affair. When he declined, the pontiff refused to bless that year's Giro d'Italia.

22
Number of stages that Coppi won in the Giro d'Italia.

The science of suffering

From their physiological capabilities through to the power they generate and the biological demands placed on their bodies, the statistics that define professional cyclists can be almost hard to believe.

80ml/min/kg

Better known as VO2 max – or maximum aerobic capacity – this long-winded but important measurement represents the number of millilitres of oxygen per kilogram of bodyweight that an athlete can utilise per minute. The figure for the best climbers will be about 80, compared to 40 for sedentary adults.

25-60g/hr

The rate at which professional cyclists need to consume carbohydrates during a race. They take most of it in through energy bars, gels and power-based fluids. A 100g energy bar will typically contain 70g of carbohydrates. A gel will have 20g-30g. For a rider, replenishing energy is complicated by the fact that the body can generally absorb only 1g of carbohydrate an hour for every 1kg of bodyweight.

2,000W-2,500W

How much power a professional sprinter generates at top speed. Most healthy men and women would struggle to produce more than 800W and 600W respectively on a bike.

5-6%

A typical pro rider's body fat on a Grand Tour. Bradley Wiggins's was said to be 4% when he won the 2012 Tour de France. A male requires a minimum of 2%-5% to regulate body temperature and protect organs.

10-15%

The percentage by which a cyclist's performance will be compromised when a stage race reaches the mountains. Altitudes of 2,000m-2,500m limit the body's ability to deliver oxygen to muscle tissue.

21

After 21 stages of a Grand Tour, a rider will begin to undergo damaging hormonal changes in which his resting cortisol and testosterone decreases. This can suppress the immune system, increase the chance of injury and raise susceptibility to mood swings.

5,500-6,000kcal

The amount of calories that a rider will consume on an especially tough stage of a Grand Tour. This is more than double the average intake that most of us require on a normal day.

450W

The average power output for a pro cyclist during a 30- to 60-minute ascent of a mountain pass. A typical, fit amateur rider would struggle to maintain the same output for more than two minutes.

10 litres

Amount of fluid that a cyclist will typically need to stay hydrated during a stage on a Grand Tour. Only a 2% drop in hydration through sweat and breathing can noticeably impair performance.

6.1W/kg

How much power a cyclist can produce per kilogram of bodyweight – their power-to-weight ratio – is a crucial measurement of their physical capability. While on an attack during a race, for example, a professional will produce about 6W/kg, more than double that of a typical competitive amateur and three times as much as a recreational cyclist.

The father of the Tour

Henri Desgrange was a record-breaking cyclist, newspaper editor and sports writer, but by far his greatest achievement was to organise the Tour de France for the first four decades of its existence.

The big idea

Though Desgrange is credited with creating the Tour, the event was not actually his idea. While editor of the cycling and car-racing newspaper *L'Auto-Velo*, his journalist Géo Lefèvre conceived of it during a crisis meeting to think up ways of halting the publication's decline in circulation.

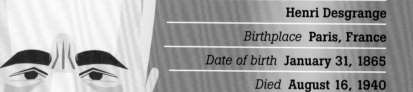

Henri Desgrange

Birthplace **Paris, France**

Date of birth **January 31, 1865**

Died **August 16, 1940**

Tour de France organiser

1903–1936

FAREWELL TOUR

Desgrange defied the wishes of his surgeon when he insisted on attending the 1936 Tour between two prostate operations. He was in such pain as a car passenger following the race that he quit on the second stage. He retired soon afterwards and died four years later at home on the Mediterranean coast.

35.525km

Desgrange was an elite endurance rider before he turned to writing and administration. He set the first recognised Hour Record in 1893, covering 35.325km at the Buffalo Velodrome in Paris.

FITNESS OBSESSION

Desgrange was a fitness enthusiast – he ran three times a week up until his death – who believed that his country had lost the Franco-Prussian War because of the poor health of the nation. He perceived the Tour not so much as a race but as social engineering that would inspire its followers to improve their physical condition. This meant that he stuck to strict rules that ensured the toughest race possible.

A NATION ENTHRALLED

L'Auto's success on the back of the Tour not only put its previously more successful rival publication *Le Velo* out of business within a year but continued to increase at a remarkable rate until it peaked in 1933:

1902: 25,000 daily readers
1903: 65,000
1908: 250,000
1923: 500,000
1933: 854,000

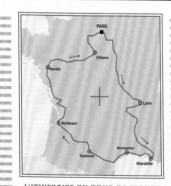

L'Auto 1903

LE TOUR DE FRANCE – LE DEPART

L'ITINERAIRE DU TOUR DE FRANCE

His rules

● Riders were banned from colluding with one another.
● They had to fix their own mechanical problems.
● He banned variable gears long after they had become popular.

What he said:

'The ideal Tour would be a Tour where only one rider managed to complete the event.'

Guide to the track

Not every cycling fan knows exactly what the purpose is of each line on a cycle track. Fortunately, *Velopedia* is here to help...

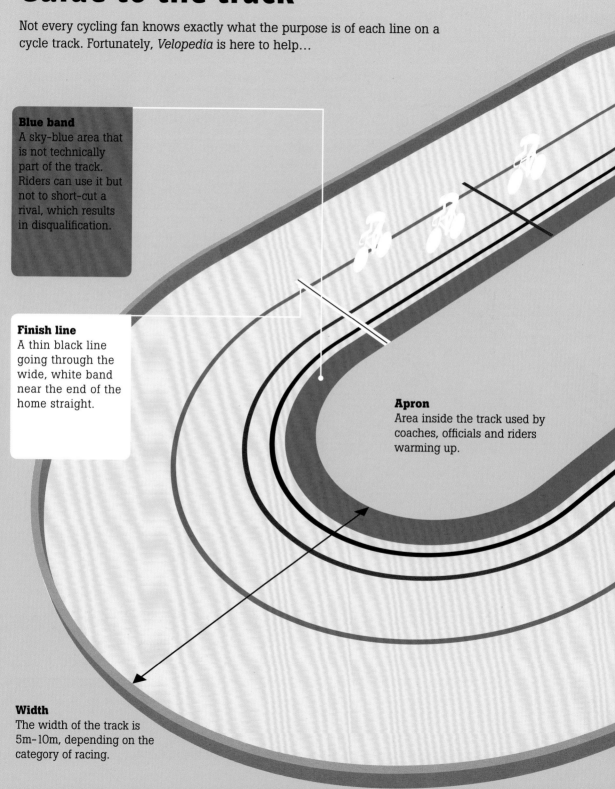

Blue band
A sky-blue area that is not technically part of the track. Riders can use it but not to short-cut a rival, which results in disqualification.

Finish line
A thin black line going through the wide, white band near the end of the home straight.

Apron
Area inside the track used by coaches, officials and riders warming up.

Width
The width of the track is 5m–10m, depending on the category of racing.

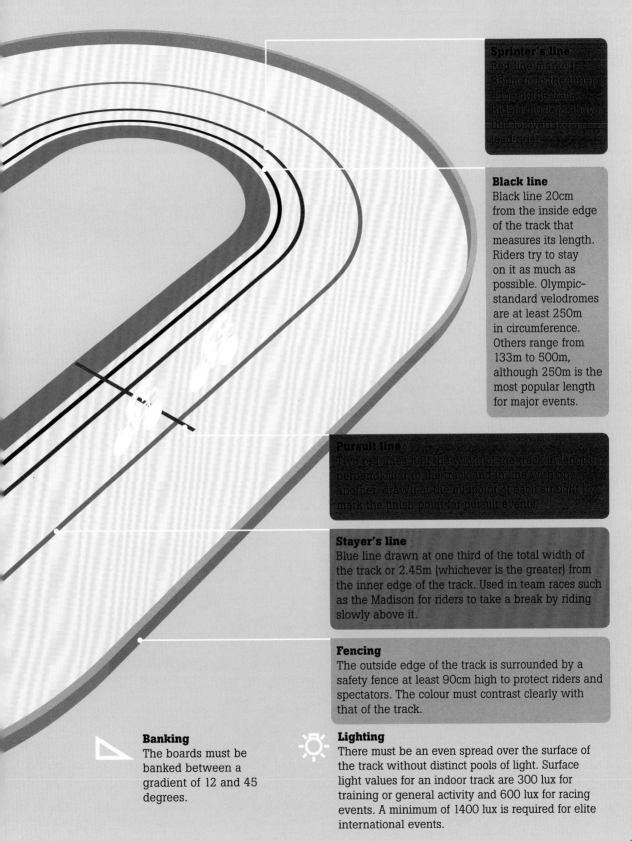

Sprinter's line
Red line marked 85cm from the inner edge of the track. Riders must go above this to overtake a lead rider.

Black line
Black line 20cm from the inside edge of the track that measures its length. Riders try to stay on it as much as possible. Olympic-standard velodromes are at least 250m in circumference. Others range from 133m to 500m, although 250m is the most popular length for major events.

Pursuit line
Two red lines half the width of the track in length, perpendicular to the track and in line with one another, drawn at the midpoint of each straight to mark the finish point for pursuit events.

Stayer's line
Blue line drawn at one third of the total width of the track or 2.45m (whichever is the greater) from the inner edge of the track. Used in team races such as the Madison for riders to take a break by riding slowly above it.

Fencing
The outside edge of the track is surrounded by a safety fence at least 90cm high to protect riders and spectators. The colour must contrast clearly with that of the track.

Banking
The boards must be banked between a gradient of 12 and 45 degrees.

Lighting
There must be an even spread over the surface of the track without distinct pools of light. Surface light values for an indoor track are 300 lux for training or general activity and 600 lux for racing events. A minimum of 1400 lux is required for elite international events.

Diets of champions

From the café-raids to slap-up breakfasts and bidons of wine, the diet of the earliest professionals would make their modern successors choke on a vitamin pill.

Pre-World War II
- With no feed stations and no team staff to replenish them on the road, riders adopted an anything-goes approach to diet and nutrition in the sport's early days.
- They would make quick stop-offs at bars and cafés en route, grabbing whatever they could lay their hands on from the menu.
- They drank alcohol throughout races to combat the pain caused by their inadequate bikes, rough road surfaces and horrendously long distances they had to ride, especially on the Grand Tours.
- It was not unusual for riders to carry with them a small bidon of wine.

1950s
- Mostly thanks to the influence of the great Fausto Coppi, riders began to adopt a more scientific approach to training and diet.
- *Il Campionissimo* was one of the first riders to advocate eating smaller, more easily digested portions at regular intervals and he began every day of a stage-race by drinking fruit and vegetable juices.
- However, many of his rivals still dismissed such forward-thinking as eccentric and stuck to eating large meals before races. A favourite dish was rice and a giant slab of steak.

1980/90s

● Understanding of diet and nutrition had vastly improved by this period but the typical diet was still different from what it is today, particularly during a long race when riders consumed cakes, sweets and sugary drinks to supplement energy levels.

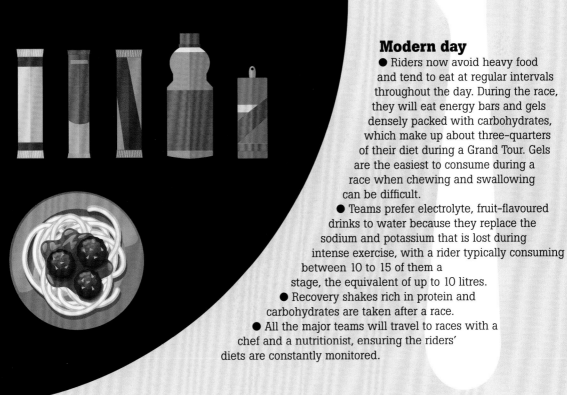

Modern day

● Riders now avoid heavy food and tend to eat at regular intervals throughout the day. During the race, they will eat energy bars and gels densely packed with carbohydrates, which make up about three-quarters of their diet during a Grand Tour. Gels are the easiest to consume during a race when chewing and swallowing can be difficult.

● Teams prefer electrolyte, fruit-flavoured drinks to water because they replace the sodium and potassium that is lost during intense exercise, with a rider typically consuming between 10 to 15 of them a stage, the equivalent of up to 10 litres.

● Recovery shakes rich in protein and carbohydrates are taken after a race.

● All the major teams will travel to races with a chef and a nutritionist, ensuring the riders' diets are constantly monitored.

ICON Beryl Burton

For sheer longevity, surely no champion cyclist can compare with Beryl Burton, the Yorkshire fruit-picker who devoted most of her life to bike racing. Though a world and national road-race champion, Burton was most given to time trials and won an incredible 71 national titles over three decades, at every distance from 10 miles to 100. That there was no professional scene for women in her time did not deter Burton: she rode simply for the love of it. Had female cyclists competed at the Olympics in her era, her palmares would surely have been even more astonishing.

25

Perhaps her most incredible achievement was to win the British Best All-Rounder competition 25 years in a row, from 1958 to 1983. For women, the BBAR ranks competitors by their average speed over the season based on their best performances in 25-, 50- and 100-mile time trials.

'When the time comes I shall get on my bike and I shall be trembling like a leaf, wondering, "Can I still go fast?" When I stop being nervous I'll stop racing.'

Burton on retirement

FAMILY RIVALRY

Burton was so obsessed with winning that she refused to shake her daughter Denise's hand on the podium when the 20-year-old Denise beat her mother to win the 1976 national road race.

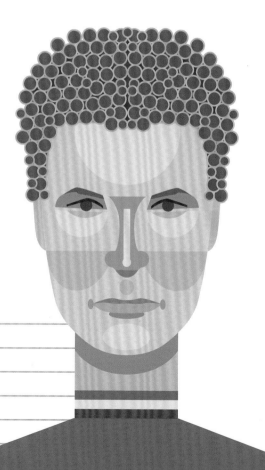

THE FACTS

Full name	**Beryl Burton**
Date of birth	**May 12, 1937**
Died	**May 8, 1995**
Birthplace	**Leeds, England**
Height	**5ft 7in (1.70m)**

THE MAJOR VICTORIES

- ○ GOLD
- ◌ SILVER
- ● BRONZE

Year	WORLD CHAMPIONSHIPS		NATIONAL CHAMPIONSHIPS	
	ROAD RACE	INDIVIDUAL PURSUIT	ROAD RACE	INDIVIDUAL PURSUIT
1959		Gold	Gold	
1960	Gold	Gold	Gold	Gold
1961	Silver		Silver	Gold
1962			Gold	Gold
1963		Gold	Gold	Gold
1964				
1965			Gold	
1966		Gold	Gold	Gold
1967	Gold	Bronze		Gold
1968		Silver	Gold	Gold
1969				
1970		Bronze	Gold	Gold
1971			Gold	Gold
1972			Gold	Gold
1973		Bronze	Gold	Gold
1974			Gold	Gold
1975		Bronze		
1976			Silver	

SWEET SUCCESS

In 1967, Burton set a national 12-hour time-trial record of 277.25 miles that surpassed the men's mark by 0.73 miles and was not bettered by a man until 1969. While setting the record, she overtook Mike McNamara, who was on his way to setting the man's record, and offered him a liquorice allsort as she sailed past him. McNamara happily ate it.

THE LAST RIDE

Burton tragically died in the saddle, suffering a heart attack while she was out delivering invitations to her 59th birthday party.

Giro d'Italia by numbers

With more than a century's worth of history, the second most prestigious bike race can be distilled down to some memorable statistics*.

2,448km

3,383km

Distance of the 1909 edition, across 8 stages.
Overall distance of the 2016 edition, across 21 stages.

70%
Percentage of winners who have been **Italian** (68 out 98 up to 2015). **Belgium** have seven winners and **Spain** six.

50.123
kilometres/hour
Stefano Allocchio's average speed when the Italian won the fastest ever stage in 1985, a 45km time trial in Foggia.

1909
First year of the race.

1931
The year that the organisers introduced the maglia rosa, or pink jersey, for the leader. It used the colour of the newspaper that sponsored it, *La Gazetta dello Sport*.

430
kilometres
Distance of longest ever stage, from Lucca to Rome, in 1914.

20.473
kilometres/hour
Arturro Ferrari's average speed when the Italian won the slowest ever stage in 1924, a 366km trek from Fiume to Verona.

222
kilometres
Distance in kilometres of the longest solo breakaway win, set by Antonio Menendez in 1976.

12
Number of starts outside Italy.

11
seconds
The closest winning margin – the difference between the winner **Fiorenzo Magni** and his fellow Italian **Ezio Cecchi** in 1948.

100%
The winning ratio of **Bernard Hinault** (France), who won each of the three editions he entered.

349,520km
Total distance the Giro has covered, which is almost the distance to the moon (370,300km).

2
Most victories in the young-rider classification. The record is shared by **Vladimir Poulnikov** (Ukraine) and **Pavel Tonkov** (Russia).

17
Number of hours that **Costante Girardengo** (Ita) needed to win the longest ever stage of the Giro in 1914. His exact time was 17hr 28min 55sec.

5
Record number of victories, shared by **Fausto Coppi** (Italy, above) **Alfredo Binda** (Italy) **Eddy Merckx** (Belgium).

4
Record number of points-jersey victories, shared by the Italians **Francesco Moser** (1976–78, 1982) and **Giuseppi Saronni** (1979, 1980, 1981, 1983)

5,325 lire
Prize money for the 1909 winner.

205,668 euros
Prize money for the 2016 winner.

12
Binda's record number of stage wins in one edition, set in the 15-stage 1927 race.

7
The Italian **Gino Bartali's** record number of victories in the mountains classification. **José Manuel Fuente** (Spa) has the second-most with the six he won in the 1970s.

42
Mario Cipollini's record number of stage wins.

78
Days that **Merckx** spent leading the Giro, a record.

*Figures correct up to 2016

A cut above

Facial hair is not ideal for a cyclist when sweat, snot and food can get stuck in it during a race, but several of the sport's most memorable nonconformists have experimented with it nonetheless.

Octave Lapize (Fra)
The winner of the 1910 Tour de France was one of the greatest riders during cycling's toughest era. He was not alone among competitors then to sport a carefully coiffured moustache.

Eugène Christophe (Fra)
The first man ever to wear the yellow jersey at the Tour, at the 1919 edition, was known as 'the Old Gaul' because he often grew a droopy, Asterix-style 'tache.

Bradley Wiggins's sideburns were so popular in 2012 that the *Daily Mirror* newspaper offered readers a cut-out-and-keep pair of them on its front page ahead of his successful attempt to win the Olympic time trial.

Sean Eadie (Aus)
The 2002 World Sprint Champion grew a beard so thick that he was renamed Captain Haddock. Perversely, the track rider was careful to shave his legs, because 'it felt great in bed'.

Marco Pantani (Ita)
Pantani's constant goatee made up for his lack of hair on top and contributed to his rebellious, piratical image in the 1990s. Memorably, he once dyed the goatee yellow while leading the Tour de France.

Frank Vandenbroucke (Bel)
The Belgian matched his goatee with a shock of long, bleached blond hair. Sadly, his wild streak led to his downfall. He fell out with riders, teams, suffered drug problems and died aged only 34.

Fabio Baldato (Ita)
Baldato maintained a goatee for all of his 17-year career. Possibly he had to keep it short and neat to satisfy directeur sportifs – who, generally, were opposed to facial hair – but when did you last see an unkempt Italian man?

Dave Zabriskie (US)
Quite what inspired Lance Armstrong's former team-mate to cultivate this handlebar 'tache and match it with chin fluff was unclear, but it looked about three decades out of fashion in 2008.

Chris Horner (US)
The ageless Horner, who was still riding as a (clean-shaven) professional in 2016 aged 44, might want to dismiss the electric-shock goatee that he sported in the early Noughties as a folly of youth.

Bradley Wiggins (GB)
Wiggins's bushy sideburns became the subject of national interest in 2012, when he anointed them his lucky charm during his golden year of winning the Tour and Olympic gold.

Luca Paolini (Ita)
The stylish winner of Gent-Wevelgem in 2015 was admired for his individualistic streak – and singular appearance – until he failed a doping test the same year and admitted to an addiction to sleeping pills.

The height of ambition

Cycling lore has it that the Grand Tours are won in the mountains, where the steepest climbs and oxygen-thin air sap the resources of riders. These passes have gained legendary status, their ramps and switchbacks feared by riders and thronged by fans. Some stand out with particular significance, their loftiness and length offering the most brutal challenge.

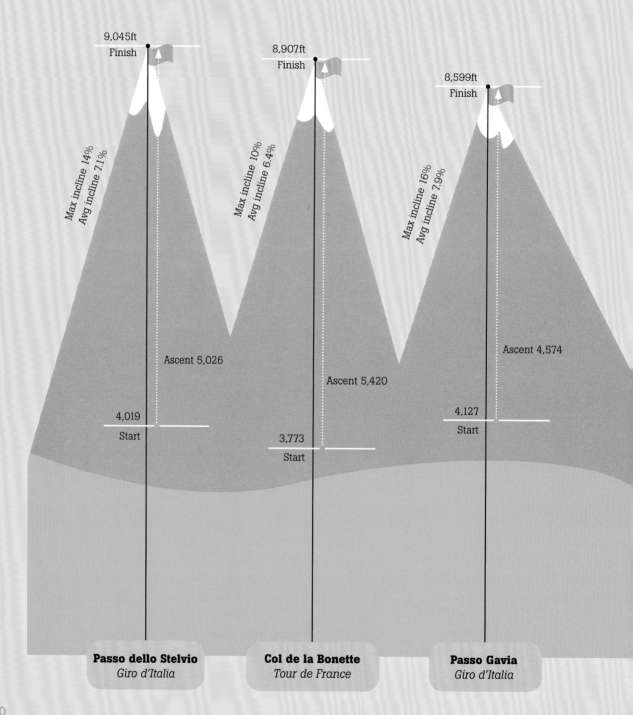

9,045ft
Finish

Max incline 14%
Avg incline 7.1%

Ascent 5,026

4,019
Start

Passo dello Stelvio
Giro d'Italia

8,907ft
Finish

Max incline 10%
Avg incline 6.4%

Ascent 5,420

3,773
Start

Col de la Bonette
Tour de France

8,599ft
Finish

Max incline 16%
Avg incline 7.9%

Ascent 4,574

4,127
Start

Passo Gavia
Giro d'Italia

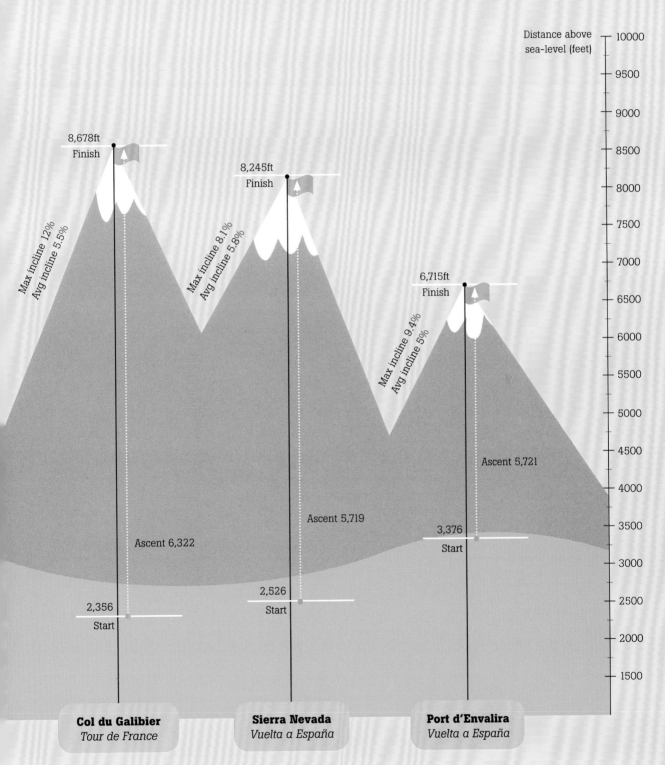

Distance above
sea-level (feet) — 10000

— 9500

— 9000

— 8500

8,678ft
Finish — 8000

8,245ft
Finish — 7500

Max incline 12%
Avg incline 5.5% — 7000

Max incline 8.1%
Avg incline 5.8% — 6500

6,715ft
Finish — 6000

Max incline 9.4%
Avg incline 5% — 5500

— 5000

Ascent 5,721 — 4500

— 4000

Ascent 6,322 — 3500

3,376
Start — 3000

Ascent 5,719

2,526
Start — 2500

2,356
Start — 2000

— 1500

Col du Galibier
Tour de France

Sierra Nevada
Vuelta a España

Port d'Envalira
Vuelta a España

'Major' Taylor

As a ground-breaking track-cycling champion and courageous hero to the African-American community, Marshall 'Major' Taylor's career is among the most remarkable in the history of his sport.

1878

Born in Indiana to a coachman who is employed in the household of the Southards, a wealthy family. Taylor's father will eventually have eight children in total.

1880

Given his first bike by the Southards. He is soon performing stunts on it for money in front of his local bike shop while dressed in a soldier's uniform, earning him the nickname 'Major'.

1896

Turns professional and quickly impresses on the track cycling scene in New York. President Theodore Roosevelt is said to be among those who take an interest in his achievements.

1898

Sets seven world records in six weeks, over 25 miles, 33 miles, five miles, .66 miles, .75 miles, one mile and two miles. His one-mile record of 1min 41sec from a standing start would stand for 28 years. He also wins 29 of the 49 races he enters during the year.

1899

Wins the world one-mile track title, becoming the first black World Cycling Champion and second black World Champion in any sport after the Canadian featherweight boxer George Dixon.

1902

Embarks on European tour, winning 40 of 57 races, defeating the champions of England, Germany and France.

1910

Retires aged 32, saying he is sick of the racism that blighted his career. Southern American states banned African-Americans from competing against white riders, rivals teamed up to conspire against Taylor, fans abused him and attempts were made to sabotage his efforts, such as scattering nails in front of his wheels.

1929

Makes a significant financial loss on his self-published autobiography. However, it would later be celebrated for its eloquent prose and Taylor's refusal to dwell on the prejudice against him.

What he said:
'Life is too short for any man to hold bitterness in his heart.'

What they said:
'Other riders would crowd him off the track, rough him up off the field, curse and threaten him. There is no telling how often he heard the "N" word, and other vicious epithets.'

Worcester journalist Albert B. Southwick

1932

Dies a pauper despite having made between $25,000 and $30,000 a year during his career. He lost huge amounts of money on bad investments and the stock market crash of 1929. He is buried in an unmarked grave in Chicago.

1948

With help from the bike-maker Frank W Schwinn, a group of former professional cyclists arrange for Taylor's remains to be exhumed and relocated to a prominent plot in an Illinois cemetery. Later, in Worcester, a monument is erected in his memory and a street is named after him.

Tainted Tours

Cyclists have doped almost since the sport began but it became illegal only in 1965. Here we chart the Tour de France champions who have since been connected to drugs.

1987 — Stephen Roche

The 1987 winner never tested positive. However, in 2000, an Italian judicial investigation concluded that a sample of his blood taken in 1993 showed traces of EPO. He was identified by a code name. Roche denied the accusation.

Pedro Delgado — 1988

The 1988 winner never tested positive for a banned substance. Did test positive for a masking agent for anabolic steroids at the 1988 Tour but it was not banned by the UCI at the time (though it was months later).

Bernard Thévenet — 1975, 1977

Admitted using sterioids when he won his two Tours in 1975 and 1977.

Floyd Landis — 2006

Tested positive, stripped of the 2006 title and banned for two years.

Jacques Anquetil — 1961–1964

Champion from 1961–4 before doping was made illegal, quoted on French television: 'Leave me in peace; everybody takes dope.'

Alberto Contador — 2008–2010

Tested positive at the 2010 Tour, stripped of that year's title and banned for two years.

Marco Pantani — 1998

Tested positive for EPO after samples from his triumphant 1998 Tour were retroactively tested in 2004.

Lucien Aimar — 1966

Champion in 1966, he tested positive for stimulants in 1969 and was banned for a month.

Lance Armstrong
1999–2005
Banned for life after admitting to doping. Was stripped of all of his seven titles.

Bjarne Riis
1996
Admitted in 2010 that he doped at the 1996 Tour, which he won.

Laurent Fignon
1983, 1984
Double Tour champion in the 1980s. Twice tested positive for banned stimulants.

Joop Zoetemelk
1980
The 1980 champion twice tested positive for stimulants. Admitted to a blood transfusion after winning a stage on the 1976 Tour though it was considered a legitimate medical aid then.

Eddy Merckx
1969–72, 1974
The winner of five Tours in the 1960s and 1970s tested positive three times. Was expelled from the 1969 Giro d'Italia after testing positive for the stimulant reactivan.

Miguel Indurain
1991–1995
Five-time winner in the 1990s never tested positive for banned substance. Did test positive for salbutamol in 1994 but UCI allowed him to use it for asthma.

Jan Ullrich
1997
The 1997 winner tested positive for amphetamines and, after he retired, admitted to blood doping during his career.

Luis Ocaña
1973
Tested positive in the 1977 Tour for the stimulant pemolin – four years after he won the title.

Felice Gimondi
1965
Tested positive in the 1968 Giro and 1975 Tour – 10 years after he won the race.

'Leave me in peace; everybody takes dope'
Jacques Anquetil

In formation

How riders respond to the wind and set up a sprint for the finish.

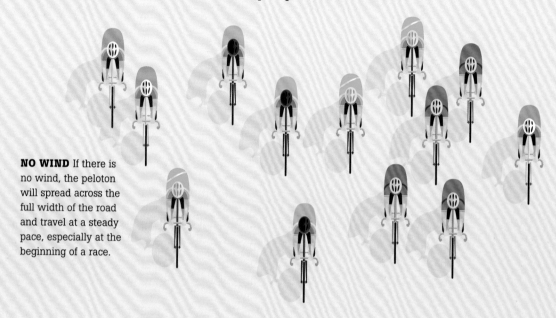

NO WIND If there is no wind, the peloton will spread across the full width of the road and travel at a steady pace, especially at the beginning of a race.

CROSSWIND In the event of a crosswind, riders form echelons in which they line up in a diagonal formation that angles away from the wind, to reduce its impact. The peloton will need to break up and form several echelons because of the limited space on the road. As ever, domestiques will tend to serve the most time at the front.

HEADWIND If the peloton meets a headwind then it will form a V or 'wedge' formation with riders taking it in turns to set the pace at the tip of the arrow. This is both aerodynamic and safe, as it gives trailing riders a view of the road ahead. Groups of birds will often form a similar formation in flight.

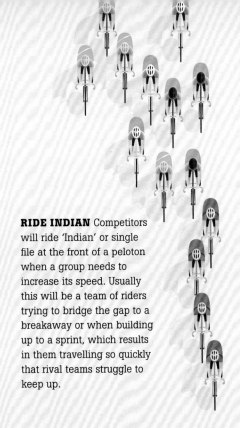

RIDE INDIAN Competitors will ride 'Indian' or single file at the front of a peloton when a group needs to increase its speed. Usually this will be a team of riders trying to bridge the gap to a breakaway or when building up to a sprint, which results in them travelling so quickly that rival teams struggle to keep up.

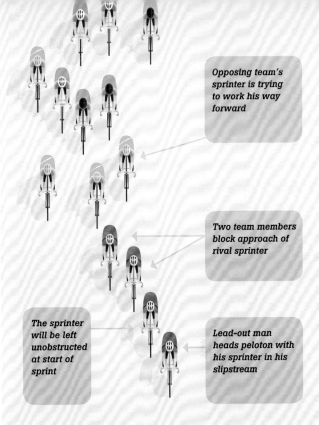

Opposing team's sprinter is trying to work his way forward

Two team members block approach of rival sprinter

The sprinter will be left unobstructed at start of sprint

Lead-out man heads peloton with his sprinter in his slipstream

↗ SPRINT TRAIN The final moments before a sprint finish can be chaotic but teams will still be employing tactics amid the mayhem. A lead-out man will front a sprint train, with the sprinter positioned on his wheel, and other team-mates behind him trying to block rival counter-attacks.

→ SPRINT FINISH In the final dash to the line, the riders at the back of the sprint train will drop their pace, again to block rivals. The lead-out man, meanwhile, will swing off to give his sprinter a clear run to the line.

ICON Jacques Anquetil

A technically brilliant, cunning and complicated *bon vivant*, Jacques Anquetil was the first man to win five Tours de France, the first to win all three Grand Tours and, by some distance, the best stage-race rider of his generation. The son of a modest Norman strawberry-grower, he was loved by purists also for his fluent, toes-down pedalling style, though his tactical outlook meant that the French public struggled to warm to him during his career, famously siding instead with his less talented rival Raymond Poulidor. This was because Anquetil rarely did more than the minimum required to win: for him, cycling was not about achieving glory but a means to ascend from peasantry to the aristocracy, a journey that was completed when he was given the Legion of Honour, the highest accolade the French state can award one of its citizens.

FAMILY AFFAIR

Anquetil had a somewhat unorthodox private life in which he married his doctor's wife, Janine, lived a ménage à trois with her and her daughter, Annie, then had an affair with Janine's daughter-in-law that produced a child.

RIDING STYLE

Anquetil's British domestique Vin Denson carried with him a comb so that his boss could fix his hair approaching the finish line and a bottle opener in case he fancied a beer from a roadside café.

What he said
'To prepare for a race there is nothing better than a good pheasant, some champagne and a woman.'

THE FACTS

Full name **Jacques Anquetil**

Nickname **Maitre Jacques**

Date of birth **January 8, 1934**

Died **November 18, 1987**

Birthplace **Mont-Saint-Aignan, Seine-Maritime, France**

Height **5ft 9½in (1.77m)**

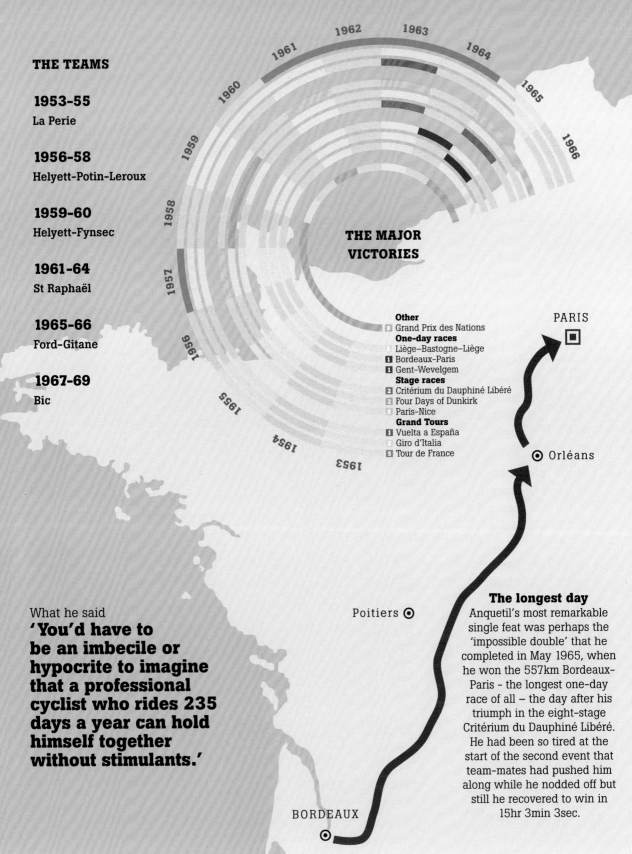

THE TEAMS

1953–55
La Perie

1956–58
Helyett-Potin-Leroux

1959–60
Helyett-Fynsec

1961–64
St Raphaël

1965–66
Ford-Gitane

1967–69
Bic

1961 1962 1963 1964 1965 1966

1960 1959 1958 1957 1956 1955 1954 1953

THE MAJOR VICTORIES

Other
⓪ Grand Prix des Nations
One-day races
☐ Liège–Bastogne–Liège
1 Bordeaux-Paris
1 Gent-Wevelgem
Stage races
2 Critérium du Dauphiné Libéré
2 Four Days of Dunkirk
5 Paris-Nice
Grand Tours
1 Vuelta a España
2 Giro d'Italia
5 Tour de France

PARIS ▣

⊙ Orléans

Poitiers ⊙

The longest day
Anquetil's most remarkable single feat was perhaps the 'impossible double' that he completed in May 1965, when he won the 557km Bordeaux-Paris - the longest one-day race of all – the day after his triumph in the eight-stage Critérium du Dauphiné Libéré. He had been so tired at the start of the second event that team-mates had pushed him along while he nodded off but still he recovered to win in 15hr 3min 3sec.

What he said
'You'd have to be an imbecile or hypocrite to imagine that a professional cyclist who rides 235 days a year can hold himself together without stimulants.'

BORDEAUX
⊙

Monument #1
Milan-San Remo

'The Spring Classic'
First edition: 1907
Distance: 295km (2016)

The first major event of the season and the longest one-day professional road race in the world, Milan-San Remo is considered the sprinters' Classic and is revered for being especially tactical because of its varied route. Established to promote the then-fading seaside resort in which it finishes, the race is the only Monument to follow a route almost identical to its original one. Italians romantically call it La Primavera, which translates literally as The Spring, because the journey from the cold of Milan to the Riviera sunshine is said to coincide with the point at which winter gives way to the new season.

Il Campionissimo

Though Eddy Merckx holds the record for Milan-San Remo victories, Costante Girardengo was for decades the rider most closely associated with the race and would have equalled Merckx's feat had he not been harshly disqualified after winning in 1915 because he had inadvertently taken a brief shortcut. As it was, Girardengo's six wins were crucial to him becoming the first rider anointed *Il Campionissimo*, 'Champion of Champions', the accolade that the Italian press famously bestows on its best riders.

45.806km/h
Fastest average speed set by Gianni Bugno when he won in 1990

22.496km/h
Winner's slowest average speed set by Gaetano Belloni in 1917

Silliest loss
In 2004, Erik Zabel lost out to Oscar Freire by 3cm after prematurely raising his arms in celebration approaching the line.

Victories by nation (up to 2016)

50	Italy	**2**	Ireland
20	Belgium		Switzerland
13	France		United Kingdom
6	Germany		Australia
5	Spain	**1**	Norway
3	Netherlands		

Passo del Turchino
'The Turchino Pass'
Average gradient: 1.4%
Maximum gradient: 6%
Length: 25.8km

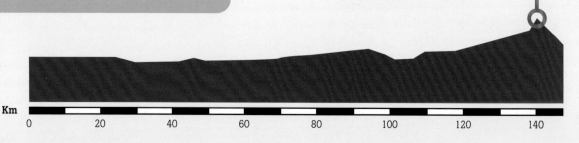

Km
0   20   40   60   80   100   120   140

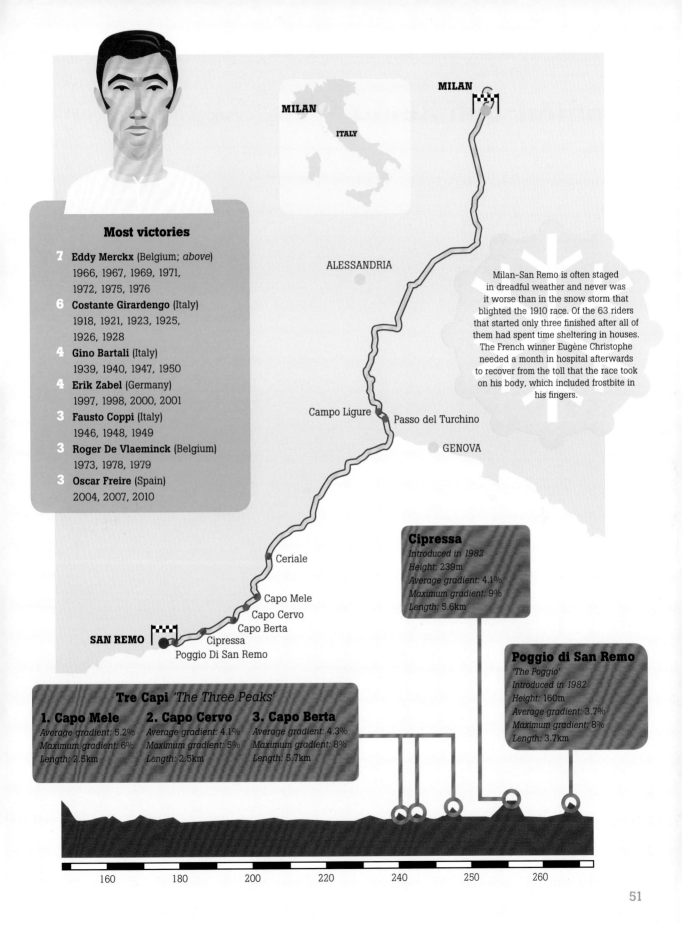

Most victories

7 **Eddy Merckx** (Belgium; *above*)
1966, 1967, 1969, 1971,
1972, 1975, 1976

6 **Costante Girardengo** (Italy)
1918, 1921, 1923, 1925,
1926, 1928

4 **Gino Bartali** (Italy)
1939, 1940, 1947, 1950

4 **Erik Zabel** (Germany)
1997, 1998, 2000, 2001

3 **Fausto Coppi** (Italy)
1946, 1948, 1949

3 **Roger De Vlaeminck** (Belgium)
1973, 1978, 1979

3 **Oscar Freire** (Spain)
2004, 2007, 2010

MILAN

MILAN
ITALY

ALESSANDRIA

Milan-San Remo is often staged
in dreadful weather and never was
it worse than in the snow storm that
blighted the 1910 race. Of the 63 riders
that started only three finished after all of
them had spent time sheltering in houses.
The French winner Eugène Christophe
needed a month in hospital afterwards
to recover from the toll that the race took
on his body, which included frostbite in
his fingers.

Campo Ligure
Passo del Turchino
GENOVA

Ceriale

Capo Mele
Capo Cervo
Capo Berta
SAN REMO
Cipressa
Poggio Di San Remo

Cipressa
Introduced in 1982
Height: 239m
Average gradient: 4.1%
Maximum gradient: 9%
Length: 5.6km

Poggio di San Remo
'The Poggio'
Introduced in 1982
Height: 160m
Average gradient: 3.7%
Maximum gradient: 8%
Length: 3.7km

Tre Capi *'The Three Peaks'*

1. Capo Mele
Average gradient: 5.2%
Maximum gradient: 6%
Length: 2.5km

2. Capo Cervo
Average gradient: 4.1%
Maximum gradient: 5%
Length: 2.5km

3. Capo Berta
Average gradient: 4.3%
Maximum gradient: 8%
Length: 5.7km

160   180   200   220   240   250   260

Tour's iconic Pyrenean climbs

Tour de France organiser Henri Desgrange was so uncertain whether riders would be able to survive in the Pyrenees when he introduced them to the race in 1910 that he stayed away from the event. He need not have worried. Their inclusion was such a success that it became a turning point for the event leading not only to the introduction of the Alps 12 months later but also ensuring that the Tour would take on epic proportions.

Gradient key
- 0-4%
- 4-7%
- 7-10%
- +10%

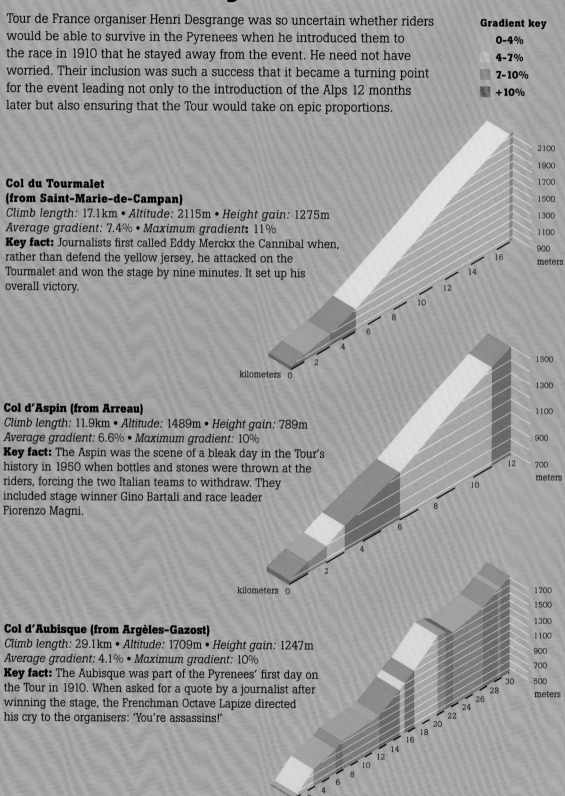

Col du Tourmalet
(from Saint-Marie-de-Campan)
Climb length: 17.1km • *Altitude:* 2115m • *Height gain:* 1275m
Average gradient: 7.4% • *Maximum gradient*: 11%
Key fact: Journalists first called Eddy Merckx the Cannibal when, rather than defend the yellow jersey, he attacked on the Tourmalet and won the stage by nine minutes. It set up his overall victory.

Col d'Aspin (from Arreau)
Climb length: 11.9km • *Altitude:* 1489m • *Height gain:* 789m
Average gradient: 6.6% • *Maximum gradient:* 10%
Key fact: The Aspin was the scene of a bleak day in the Tour's history in 1950 when bottles and stones were thrown at the riders, forcing the two Italian teams to withdraw. They included stage winner Gino Bartali and race leader Fiorenzo Magni.

Col d'Aubisque (from Argèles-Gazost)
Climb length: 29.1km • *Altitude:* 1709m • *Height gain:* 1247m
Average gradient: 4.1% • *Maximum gradient:* 10%
Key fact: The Aubisque was part of the Pyrenees' first day on the Tour in 1910. When asked for a quote by a journalist after winning the stage, the Frenchman Octave Lapize directed his cry to the organisers: 'You're assassins!'

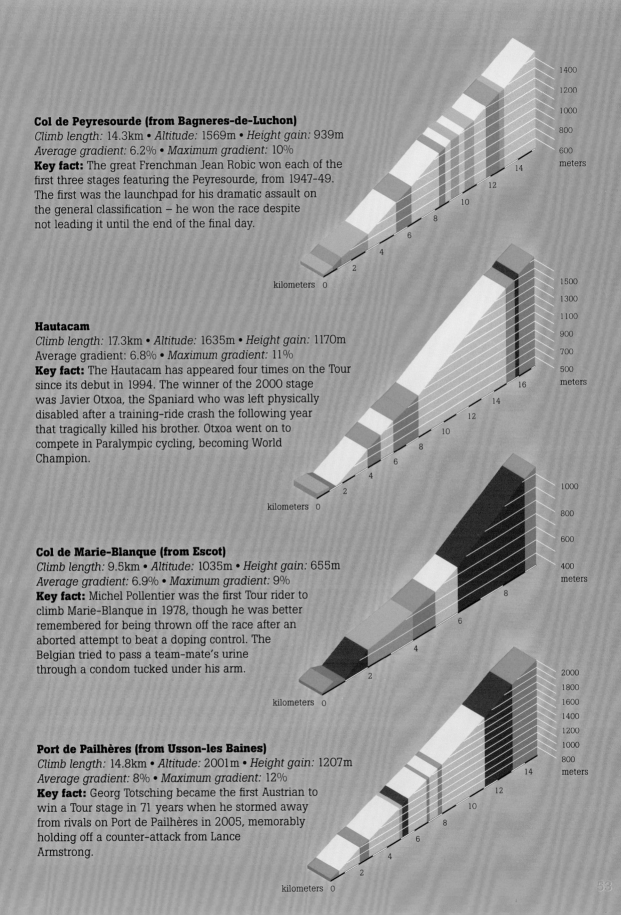

Col de Peyresourde (from Bagneres-de-Luchon)
Climb length: 14.3km • *Altitude:* 1569m • *Height gain:* 939m
Average gradient: 6.2% • *Maximum gradient:* 10%
Key fact: The great Frenchman Jean Robic won each of the
first three stages featuring the Peyresourde, from 1947-49.
The first was the launchpad for his dramatic assault on
the general classification – he won the race despite
not leading it until the end of the final day.

Hautacam
Climb length: 17.3km • *Altitude:* 1635m • *Height gain:* 1170m
Average gradient: 6.8% • *Maximum gradient:* 11%
Key fact: The Hautacam has appeared four times on the Tour
since its debut in 1994. The winner of the 2000 stage
was Javier Otxoa, the Spaniard who was left physically
disabled after a training-ride crash the following year
that tragically killed his brother. Otxoa went on to
compete in Paralympic cycling, becoming World
Champion.

Col de Marie-Blanque (from Escot)
Climb length: 9.5km • *Altitude:* 1035m • *Height gain:* 655m
Average gradient: 6.9% • *Maximum gradient:* 9%
Key fact: Michel Pollentier was the first Tour rider to
climb Marie-Blanque in 1978, though he was better
remembered for being thrown off the race after an
aborted attempt to beat a doping control. The
Belgian tried to pass a team-mate's urine
through a condom tucked under his arm.

Port de Pailhères (from Usson-les Baines)
Climb length: 14.8km • *Altitude:* 2001m • *Height gain:* 1207m
Average gradient: 8% • *Maximum gradient:* 12%
Key fact: Georg Totsching became the first Austrian to
win a Tour stage in 71 years when he stormed away
from rivals on Port de Pailhères in 2005, memorably
holding off a counter-attack from Lance
Armstrong.

The maglia rosa

The coveted pink jersey is given to the leader of the general classification after each stage of the Giro d'Italia, but only the champion is said to 'win' it.

8

4

0

13

19

Francesco Moser (Ita) wore pink in eight different Giros, more than any other rider.

Number of riders who have worn the leader's jersey from the second stage until the finish.

Costante Girardengo *(Ita)*, *10 stages, 1919*
Alfredo Binda *(Ita)*, *15 stages, 1927*
Eddy Merckx *(Bel)*, *20 stages, 1973*
Gianni Bugno *(Ita)*, *21 stages, 1990*

Italo Zilioli (Ita) finished runner-up three years in succession – from 1964 to 1966 – without ever once wearing the maglia rosa.

Number of riders who won the maglia rosa without winning a stage of the same Giro.

José Manuel Fuente (Spa) spent 19 days in pink without ever winning the Giro.

1931

The pink jersey was introduced in 1931, 22 years after the first Giro.

1940

Italy's Campionissimo **Fausto Coppi** was 20 years, 158 days old when, in 1940, he became the youngest winner of the pink jersey.

1950

Hugo Koblet, of Switzerland, was the first non-Italian to win the maglia rosa in 1950, in the 33rd edition of the Giro.

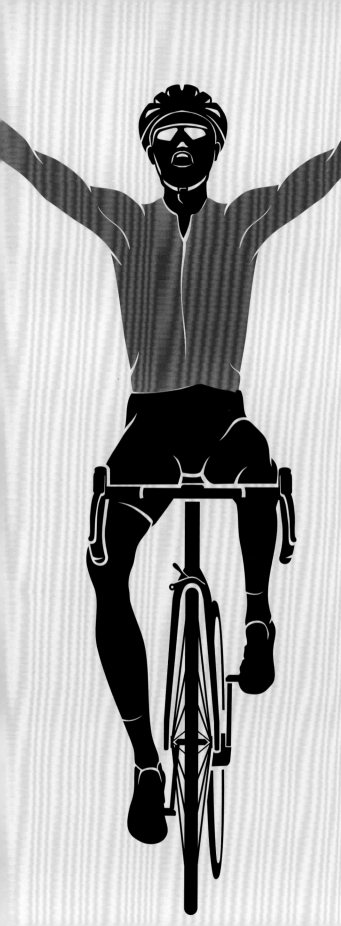

MOST DAYS IN PINK

77 Eddy Merckx (Bel), 1968–1974
65 Alfredo Binda (Ita), 1925–1933
50 Francesco Moser (Ita), 1976–1985
48 Giuseppe Saronni (Ita), 1979–1986
42 Gino Bartali (Ita), 1936–1947
42 Jacques Anquetil (Fra), 1959–1967
31 Bernard Hinault (Fra), 1940–1954
31 Fausto Coppi (Ita), 1980–1985
29 Miguel Indurain (Spa), 1992–1993
26 Costante Girardengo (Ita), 1919–1926
16 Roberto Visentini (Ita), 1980–1987

1955

The near-veteran Italian **Fiorenzo Magni** was 34 years, 180 days old when he became the oldest winner of the maglia rosa in 1955.

*Figures correct up to and including the 2016 Giro.

Inside the super-truck ...

Both the Team Sky truck and their coach were the envy of the peloton when they pitched up at the Tour de France. No wonder, given their impressive specification and how much they managed to fit inside.

90
Tubular tyres
Per stage race. A leading rider is likely to have a new pair for each stage.

1
Kitchen
Separate room with sink, washer and dryer.

40
Cassettes
Ratios: 11–25, 11–28, 11–32.

2
Volvo FH500 trucks
General manager Dave Brailsford and his team bring two of the vehicles to a major race.

1
Awning
Mechanics can also work outside, beneath the awning, when the weather is fine.

27
Bikes
One racing bike plus two spares for each rider on a Grand Tour team.

2
Work stations
The sides and back of the truck extend when stationary to create room for mechanics to work at two bike-stands. There are also two work benches.

... and features of the super-bus

Six seat belts

Six-person dinette

AIR CONDITIONING

Electric entrance step with awning

FIXED DOUBLE BED OVER THE CAB

WASHROOM WITH SEPARATE SHOWER

Large U-shaped lounge area which makes two single beds or a large double

NEW CLUTCH 2,000 MILES AGO

ONE-YEAR ANTI-DAMP WARRANTY

PANORAMIC ROOF LIGHT

FRIDGE, OVEN/GRILL AND FOUR-BURNER HOB

CRUISE CONTROL

SINK AND ELECTRONIC FLUSH TOILET

LARGE BIKE/MOTORBIKE RACK

DOUBLE FLOOR WITH HUGE STORAGE CAPACITY

NO RIPS OR TEARS

SIX-SPEED GEARBOX

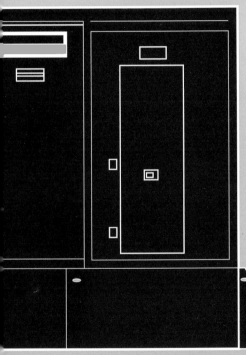

4
Mechanics
Sky bring the most personnel to a Grand Tour. They take three mechanics to a Classic and two to a less prestigious stage race.

50
Wheel sets
Including Shimano C50s, C35s, C24s and C75s, giving riders options for different terrain. As a team sponsor, Shimano is on hand to supplement their wheel supply, too.

1,400
Bidons
Riders throw bottles away during the race.

8
Groupsets
Enough to set up a further eight bikes in an emergency.

The African powerhouse

The story of cycling in Eritrea was rarely told until its most famous son, Daniel Teklehaimanot, enjoyed success at the 2015 Tour de France. This was a shame because the tale of the sport's rise from the preserve of fascist colonialists in the east African country to being an 'unofficial, state-sanctioned religion', as the *Economist* described it, is an intriguing one.

1890	1898	1930	1939	1946
Italy formally announces the creation of Italian Eritrea several years after its colonialists began settling in the region.	According to record, the first bicycle is sighted in the coastal city of Massawa.	Cycling clubs are set up by the ruling Italian elite, with the first race taking place in the capital Asmara in 1937. Segregationist policies under the rule of Italian dictator Mussolini, however, prevent Eritreans from taking part. The locals respond by forming their own clubs and races.	The Italian administration finally allows Italians and Eritreans to compete in the same event, known as 'the trial of strength'. **Ghebremariam Ghebru** shatters colonial myths about Eritrean – and African – inferiority by winning the race.	The Tour of Eritrea is held for the first time. The Italian **Nunzio Barilà** beats 33 rivals to win the five-stage race. The race is held again the following year then abandoned because of an emerging guerilla war.

THE TOUR OF ERITREA 2016

- Start and finish city
- Start city
- Finish city
- Two-way stage
- One-way stage
- Coach travel

100 km

AFRICA

ERITREA

ERITREA'S CYCLING HISTORY

1960-1970	1991	2001	2009	2015

1960-1970

The sport continued to thrive despite growing political instability and decades of intermittent war. Several strong riders emerged, such as the Olympians **Tekeste Woldu** and **Yemane Negassi**, though they were still outcast by the ruling regime and had to represent Ethopia internationally.

1991

Eritrea gains independence, giving the indigenous population more freedom to enjoy cycling. Many more start to take up the sport competitively. The number of clubs quickly grows. By now, cycling is the primary means of transport in a country with a patchy, at best, petrol supply.

2001

The Tour of Eritrea is revived to celebrate ten years of independence. The Etritrean rider **Habte Weldesimon** wins an extremely challenging 10-stage event covering 700km. On a course that crosses desert, mountain regions and coastal plains, it is now by far the country's most popular sporting event, with thousands of fans lining the roads to watch.

2009

The UCI officially recognises the Tour of Eritrea, giving it category-two status.

2015

Daniel Teklehaimanot and **Merhawi Kudus** become both the first Eritreans and the first black Africans to start the Tour de France, racing for South African team MTN–Qhubeka. Teklehaimanot would famously go on to wear the polka-dot jersey for three stages of the race.

NATIONAL ICON

Daniel Teklehaimanot is the most successful of the emerging crop of Eritrean riders.

In 2012, he became both the first Eritrean to represent the country at an Olympics in a sport other than athletics and the first of his countrymen to compete in the Vuelta a España.

In 2015, he wore the climber's jersey from stages six to nine of his first Tour de France.

Date of birth: **Nov 10, 1988**

Team: **Dimension Data**

African road-race titles: **1**

African individual time-trial titles: **4**

African team time-trial titles: **5**

Critérium du Dauphiné mountains classification: **2015, 2016**

ICON Eddy Merckx

Put simply, the greatest cyclist who ever lived and one who dominated his sport like no one has ever done, winning a record 11 Grand Tour titles, 17 Monuments and three World Road Race titles, as well as breaking the hour record. The son of a grocer from a Brussels suburb, Merckx actually grew up as a shy young man and, as a result, was mocked by other riders when he first emerged on the competitive racing scene in the 1960s. With the ability to sprint and climb with devastating success, however, and being inclined to destroy the toughest fields on courageous lone breakaways, he soon silenced their barbs and went on to clock 525 triumphs in total. His voracious appetite for victory was such that his contemporaries nicknamed him the Cannibal.

What he said
'Don't buy upgrades, ride up grades'

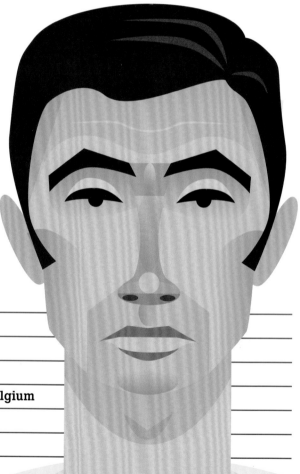

THE FACTS

Full name **Edouard Louis Joseph Merckx**

Nickname **The Cannibal**

Date of birth **June 17, 1945**

Birthplace **Meensel-Kiezegem, Brabant, Belgium**

Height **6ft 1in (1.85m)**

Weight **11st 9lb (74kg)**

Discipline **Road and track**

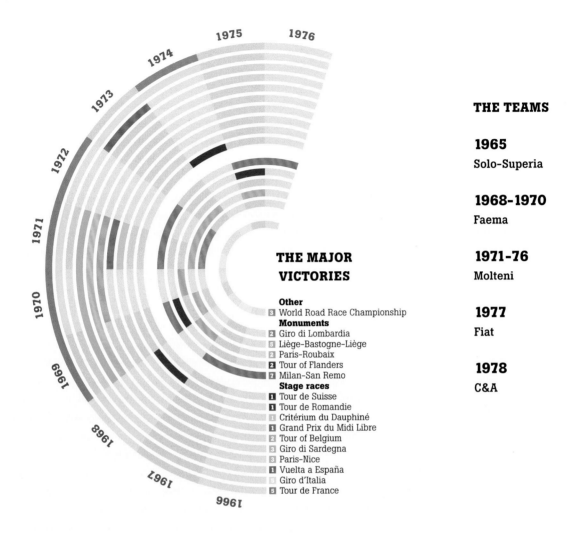

THE TEAMS

1965
Solo-Superia

1968-1970
Faema

1971-76
Molteni

1977
Fiat

1978
C&A

THE MAJOR VICTORIES

Other
3 World Road Race Championship
Monuments
2 Giro di Lombardia
5 Liège-Bastogne-Liège
2 Paris-Roubaix
2 Tour of Flanders
7 Milan-San Remo
Stage races
1 Tour de Suisse
1 Tour de Romandie
1 Critérium du Dauphiné
1 Grand Prix du Midi Libre
2 Tour of Belgium
3 Giro di Sardegna
3 Paris-Nice
1 Vuelta a España
5 Giro d'Italia
5 Tour de France

THE HOUR-RECORD BIKE

In Mexico City, on October 25, 1972, Merckx broke the Hour Record on a bespoke bike that was built by his friend Ernesto Colnago, the celebrated Italian bike-builder.

Weight **12lbs 1⅝oz**
Frame **Columbus special record tubing**
Rims **Fiamme Ergal**
Chain **Regina Record**
Saddle **Selle Royal**
Pedals **Campagnolo Record SL Strada**
Handlebars **Cinelli Campione del Mondo**
Tyres **Clement Seta Pista**

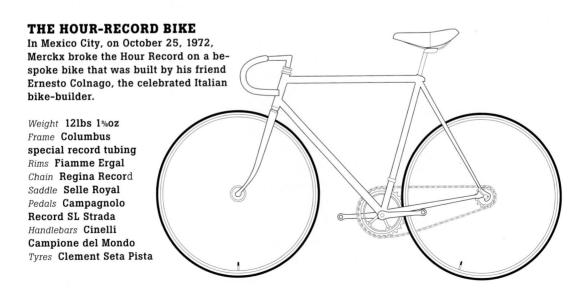

Six-day 'circus'

Six-day track meetings are among the oldest forms of competition in cycling and have had a tumultuous history, from their earliest days as physically hazardous tests of endurance to their golden age from the 1930s to the 1980s, when they were among the most lucrative events in the sport. Today they offer some of the most entertaining spectacles on the track and serve as a link to an important part of cycling heritage.

1878
The first six-day race was held at the Agricultural Hall in Islington, north London, when a professional called David Stanton won a bet of £100 after claiming he could ride 1,000 miles on the track in six successive days, using a 'high-wheeler' or penny farthing. He completed the task in 73 hours.

STATESIDE SUCCESS
The event was popularised soon after the first one was staged at New York's Madison Square Gardens in 1891 and especially once riders started competing 24 hours a day with the help of stimulants. The *New York Times* wrote: 'An athletic contest in which participants "go queer" in their heads, and strain their powers until their faces become hideous with the tortures that rack them, is not sport. It is brutality.'

MOST SUCCESSFUL RIDERS

1. Patrick Sercu (Belgium 1961–1983)
Victories: **223** Races: **223**

2. Danny Clark (Australia 1974–1997)
Victories: **74** Races: **235**

3. René Pijnen (Netherlands 1969–1987)
Victories: **72** Races: **233**

4. Peter Post (Netherlands 1956–1972)
Victories: **65** Races: **155**

5. Bruno Risi (Switzerland 1991–2008)
Victories: **61** Races: **178**

'It wasn't all fixed but the big teams would look after themselves — it would nearly always come down to a shoot-out between them on the final evening. But you needed to be very strong, very aware of what was going on and a bit lucky. Even then it was very, very hard to win. That's my main memory of them: the best teams would just beat you up.'
Rob Hayles, British track rider

THE CIRCUS

Though riders were not always happy about it, six-day events have been widely known as a 'circus'. This was partly because of the entertainment staged, with funfairs, nightclubs and concerts taking place at them. However, it was also because some of the races were said to have been 'fixed' by the top riders, and drugs were widely used by the exhausted competitors for decades.

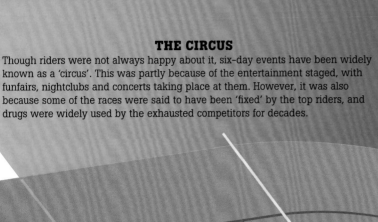

THE RULES

While riders once competed alone and over 24 hours, now they ride in pairs, taking in turns to race, and typically from 6pm to 2am across six nights. The overall winner is the team that completes the most laps of the track during the event. In the event of a draw, teams are separated by points won in intermediate competitions such as the points race, the sprint, the elimination race and time trials. The madison – a relay-style event named after Madison Square Garden – is the cornerstone event, being staged twice a session.

Guide to the Grand Tour jerseys

What the points-classification leaders wear in cycling's three biggest races.

White jersey
Leader in the young rider classification
Introduced in 1975 (although the white jersey was not worn between 1989 and 1999). The criteria for a 'young rider' has changed over the years, but most recently means those aged under 26.

Green jersey
Leader in the points classification
Introduced in 1953 to celebrate the 50th anniversary of the Tour. Green was chosen for the sprinter's jersey because the sponsor was a lawn-mower producer.

White jersey
Leader in the young rider classification
This competition was introduced in 1976 but suspended in 1994 and did not return until 2010. It is open to any rider under the age of 25.

Red jersey
Leader in the points classification
The sprinters' competition started in 1958, with the leader being given a red jersey from 1967 to 1969. He then wore a mauve version from 1970 until 2010 when it reverted back to *maglia rosso*.

Green jersey
Leader in the points classification
The sprinters' competition began in 1945 but was staged for just one year and did not return until 1955 and has taken place every year since then. The jersey was previously blue with yellow-fish emblems because it was sponsored by Spain's fishing and marine industry.

Blue white polka-dot jersey
Leader in the mountains classification
The competition was established in 1935, with the leader wearing green until 2005 and orange from 2006 until 2010. It took on its current pattern – similar to the Tour's equivalent – after that.

Tour de France

Giro d'Italia

Vuelta a España

Red jersey
Leader in the overall classification
The Vuelta's most prized jersey changed to red in 2010 at the behest of its sponsor Ahorre Energía (Save Energy), the government agency. Previously it had, at different times, been gold, orange, white and yellow.

Pink jersey
Leader in the overall classification
Introduced in 1931. The colour was chosen to reflect the pink paper of the newspaper that created the Giro, *La Gazzetta dello Sport*.

Blue jersey
Leader in the mountains classification
The climbers' competition began in 1933. From 1974 until 2011, the leader wore green, but it then changed to blue to reflect the branding of Banca Mediolanum, the Italian bank that sponsored it.

Red Polka–dot jersey
Leader in the mountains classification
Introduced in 1975 – although the climbers' competition began in 1933. The pattern was picked by the sponsor, a chocolate-bar manufacturer, whose wrappers were similarly designed.

Yellow jersey
Leader in the general classifications
Introduced in 1919. The colour is thought to have been inspired by the yellow newsprint of *L'Auto* the publication that organised the Tour.

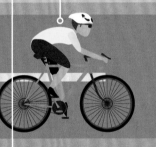

Tour de France

Giro d'Italia

Vuelta a España

Head cases

From heavy pith helmets to those made of leather straps and on to the modern, aerodynamic design, cyclists' headwear has changed immeasurably since the sport emerged.

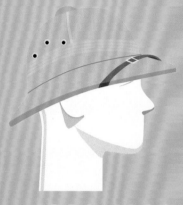

1880-1900
Pith helmets
Some cyclists on 'high-wheelers' or penny farthings wore pith helmets to combat the problem of frequent head injuries, even though pith was a crushable material and lasted only one major impact.

1900-1970
Leather look
Riders started using helmets – known as 'crash hats' – made of strips of leather-covered padding at the turn of the century. The 1960s version, the so-called Danish, was considered very stylish but offered little protection.

1910-1970
Hats off
While some riders still used the crash hats, for decades, others wore nothing more on their heads than the peaked caps that remain popular among cyclists seeking that retro look today. On hot days, some would stuff a cabbage leaf into the cap to help keep cool.

1970-1980
Plastic shells
They were made from polystyrene shells and quickly became popular.

1990–2000

Strike action

Helmets became moulded and increasingly lightweight through the 1980s, but the peloton still felt compelled to go on strike during the 1991 Paris-Nice race to protest successfully against the UCI making hard-shell helmets compulsory. It led to great strides being taken in their safety and comfort, with the introduction of thinner plastic shells crucial to those improvements.

2003

Helmets rule

Helmets were finally made compulsory in 2003, after the tragic deaths of the Italian Olympic champion Fabio Casartelli, in 1995, and the Kazakh Andrei Kivilev. Vastly improved ventilation as well as new aerodynamic technology meant that there was little resistance to the ruling.

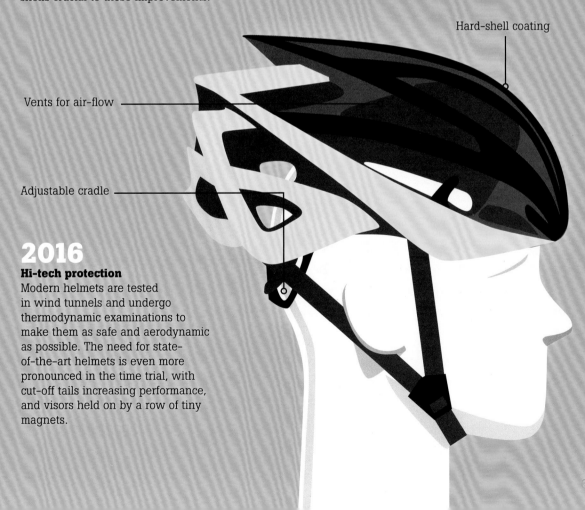

Hard-shell coating

Vents for air-flow

Adjustable cradle

2016

Hi-tech protection

Modern helmets are tested in wind tunnels and undergo thermodynamic examinations to make them as safe and aerodynamic as possible. The need for state-of-the-art helmets is even more pronounced in the time trial, with cut-off tails increasing performance, and visors held on by a row of tiny magnets.

On pain

Cyclists have a special relationship with pain. In almost no other sport are competitors required to suffer so deeply for so long to reach their goals. It has led to some memorable insights into the experience.

'The Tour de France is Calvary. Worse than that, because the road to the cross has only 14 stations and ours has 15. We suffer from the start to the end.'
Henri Pélissier, winner of the 1923 Tour

'Cycling isn't a game, it's a sport. Tough, hard and unpitying, and it requires great sacrifices. One plays football, or tennis, or hockey. One doesn't play at cycling.'
Jean de Gribaldy, French professional 1945-1954, directeur sportif 1964-1986

'It never gets easier, you just go faster.'
Greg LeMond

'If I'd any idea how much I was going to suffer, I'd never have done it. No chance.'
Chris Boardman after breaking the hour record

'You have to put up with, and face down, the physical pain and turn a deaf ear to your screaming body. You can get 30% more power out of yourself if you're able to inflict such terrible punishment on yourself. I sometimes thought of my father [a stonemason], and I would tell myself that he had suffered worse things than me in his childhood.'
Jacques Anquetil on time trials

'You can say that climbers suffer the same as the other riders, but they suffer in a different way. You feel the pain, but you're glad to be there.'
Richard Virenque

'I still feel that variable gears are only for people over 45. Isn't it better to triumph by the strength of your muscles than by the artifice of a derailleur? We are getting soft. Give me a fixed gear!'
Henri Desgrange, former French professional and the first organiser of the Tour de France

'Training is like fighting with a gorilla. You don't stop when you're tired. You stop when the gorilla is tired.'
Greg Henderson, New Zealander who rode the 2016 season with Lotto-Soudal

'When it's hurting you, that's when you can make a difference.'
Eddy Merckx

'Cycling is suffering.'
Fausto Coppi

'Sprinters suffer so much during the race just to get to the finish. They hang on for dear life in the climbs but then, in the final kilometres, they are transformed and do amazing things. It's not their force per se that impresses me, but rather the renaissance they experience, seeing them suffer only to be reborn.'
Miguel Indurain

'I figured that I would hurt everyone else before I hurt myself. In the morning I would say to myself, 'I'm going to beat that guy by five minutes.' Of course, I suffered during the race, but at the start it was like putting a video in the machine: I could see my victory in advance.'
Bernard Hinault

'I check the weather, I put on my gear, I go out and do my spin, then when I'm back I decide if it was too wet or not.'
Sean Kelly, Ireland's former world No1

Tour's great Alpine climbs

When the Alps were first introduced to the Tour de France in 1911, the prospect of crossing mountain passes barely passable on foot seemed far-fetched, but they have gone on to become a crucial fixture on the Tour route and the site of many of the most memorable battles in the sport.

Gradient key

0-4% 4-7% 7-10% +10%

Col de l'Iseran (from Val d'Isère)
Climb length: 16km • *Altitude:* 2764m • *Height gain:* 960m
Average gradient: 5.5% • *Maximum gradient:* 8%
Key fact: The first Tour rider to ascend the Iseran was the Belgian Felicien Vervaecke in 1938. He went on to become Eddy Merckx's first coach.

Galibier (from Valloire – and over Col du Tèlègraphe)
Climb length: 18km • *Altitude:* 2646m • *Height gain:* 1216m
Average gradient: 6.9% • *Maximum gradient:* 10%
Key fact: The Galibier was first used on the Tour in 1911. Only three of the 50 riders who finished the stage managed not to dismount when ascending it.

Izoard (from Guillestre)
Climb length: 31.7km • *Altitude:* 2360m • *Height gain:* 1438m
Average gradient: 6.9% • *Maximum gradient:* 7%
Key fact: Silhouettes of Tour greats Louison Bobet and Fausto Coppi have been attached to a rock two kilometres from the summit.

Col de la Croix de Fer (from Saint-Jean-de-Maurienne)
Climb length: 27.5km • *Altitude:* 2064m • *Height gain:* 1291m
Average gradient: 4.7% • *Maximum gradient:* 12%
Key fact: The 2015 Tour was the 17th on which the Croix de Fer has appeared. Perhaps the most memorable occasion in recent times was Gert-Jan Theunisse's solo ascent of it in 1989, part of a 130km solo attack that earnt the Dutchman the stage victory.

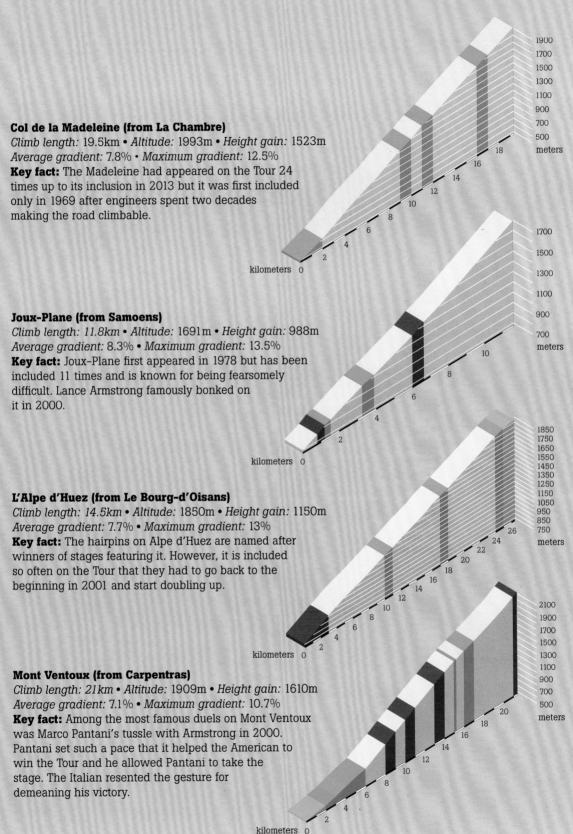

Col de la Madeleine (from La Chambre)

Climb length: 19.5km • *Altitude:* 1993m • *Height gain:* 1523m
Average gradient: 7.8% • *Maximum gradient:* 12.5%

Key fact: The Madeleine had appeared on the Tour 24 times up to its inclusion in 2013 but it was first included only in 1969 after engineers spent two decades making the road climbable.

Joux-Plane (from Samoens)

Climb length: 11.8km • *Altitude:* 1691m • *Height gain:* 988m
Average gradient: 8.3% • *Maximum gradient:* 13.5%

Key fact: Joux-Plane first appeared in 1978 but has been included 11 times and is known for being fearsomely difficult. Lance Armstrong famously bonked on it in 2000.

L'Alpe d'Huez (from Le Bourg-d'Oisans)

Climb length: 14.5km • *Altitude:* 1850m • *Height gain:* 1150m
Average gradient: 7.7% • *Maximum gradient:* 13%

Key fact: The hairpins on Alpe d'Huez are named after winners of stages featuring it. However, it is included so often on the Tour that they had to go back to the beginning in 2001 and start doubling up.

Mont Ventoux (from Carpentras)

Climb length: 21km • *Altitude:* 1909m • *Height gain:* 1610m
Average gradient: 7.1% • *Maximum gradient:* 10.7%

Key fact: Among the most famous duels on Mont Ventoux was Marco Pantani's tussle with Armstrong in 2000. Pantani set such a pace that it helped the American to win the Tour and he allowed Pantani to take the stage. The Italian resented the gesture for demeaning his victory.

Grand Tour flare-ups

With tensions running high on the Grand Tours and riders competing at their physical and emotional limits, it is hardly surprising that they occasionally lash out at rivals, team-mates and even the odd fan. Here are six of the most infamous episodes.

MERCKX DOWN AND OUT

Stage 14 – 1975 Tour de France
Eddy Merckx v drunk spectator

Perhaps the most infamous punch in cycling. Merckx was leading the race and in pursuit of a record sixth title when he attempted to chase the home favourite Bernard Thévenet on the final climb, only for a drunken fan to punch him in the kidney. The assault left the Belgian badly winded and helped Thévenet to go on and win the Tour.

FAN KO'D

Stage 14 – 2001 Giro d'Italia
Vladimir Belli v Gilberto Simoni's nephew

The Italian Belli floored a spectator with an expertly timed right hook on the Santa Barbara pass. Belli, who was chasing victory, argued that he felt intimidated by fans on the crucial final climb of the stage, but he was still disqualified. It did not help his case that he had punched the nephew of his compatriot Simoni, who was race leader at the time.

DRUG RUN

Stage 19 – 2011 Tour de France
Alberto Contador v fan in fancy dress

On the pivotal stage of the race, and with Contador's hopes of overall victory fading, he took umbrage with a spectator who had dressed up as a blood-bag wielding doctor and chased the Spaniard on Alpe d'Huez. Contador, who had failed a drugs test a year earlier – and was eventually banned – responded with a glancing blow to the chin.

**Ivan Rovny v
Gianluca Brambilla**

BREAKAWAY BUST UP

Punch-ups usually occur in sprint finishes or in tightly bunched pelotons, but the tension between this pair turned nasty while they were in a breakaway, with the Russian Rovny upsetting his Italian rival for supposedly disrupting the pace of the group. Both men were eventually kicked out of the race for hitting and elbowing one another.

ROAD RAGE

Stage 21 – 2000 Tour de France
Jeroen Blijlevens v Bobby Julich

Dutchman Blijlevens was infuriated when he thought Julich blocked him during a sprint finish on the final stage, and retaliated after the finish by taking a swing at the bemused American, who immediately fought back. The race organisers sided with the American, giving Blijlevens a hefty fine and disqualifying him from the Tour.

WRESTLE MANIA

Stage 6 – 2010 Tour de France
Rui Costa v Carlos Barredo

Few bust-ups were as dramatic as this one. Enraged by what Rui Costa insisted was an intentional elbow to the gut near the end of the stage, the Portuguese rider released his front wheel upon finishing, charged at Barredo and attempted to strike the Spaniard with it. The men exchanged a flurry of punches and then wrestled on the floor.

ICON Alberto Contador

The most decorated modern rider, Contador secured his place among the all-time greats when he became the youngest ever cyclist to win all three Grand Tours, an achievement he completed in a record-quick 14 months. He is known best for his superb climbing prowess and ability to blow the peloton apart with punchy attacks, which invariably would be executed in his signature 'dancing' pedalling style. A doping controversy stained his reputation but the modest Madrilenian remained among the most respected riders in the sport.

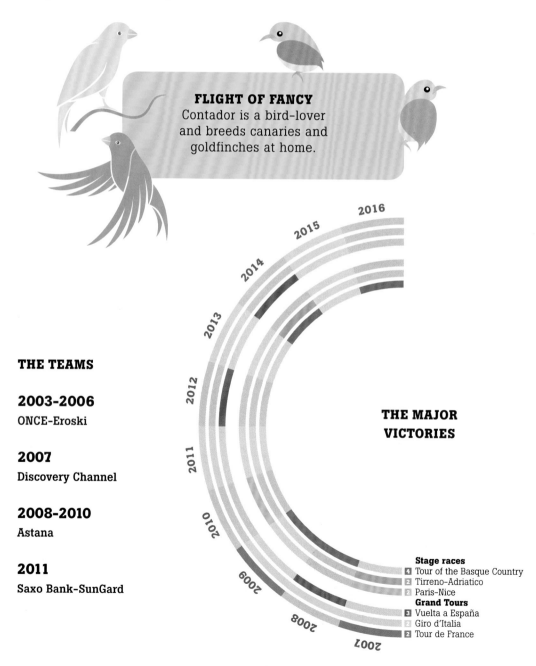

FLIGHT OF FANCY
Contador is a bird-lover and breeds canaries and goldfinches at home.

THE TEAMS

2003-2006
ONCE-Eroski

2007
Discovery Channel

2008-2010
Astana

2011
Saxo Bank-SunGard

THE MAJOR VICTORIES

Stage races
- 4 Tour of the Basque Country
- 2 Tirreno-Adriatico
- 2 Paris-Nice

Grand Tours
- 3 Vuelta a España
- 2 Giro d'Italia
- 2 Tour de France

> **'The pain reached a level and stayed there. It was so bad it couldn't get any worse.'**
> Contador on dislocating his shoulder on stage six of the 2015 Giro, which he won.

RAW DEAL
After a long legal battle, Contador was found guilty in 2012 of accidentally consuming clenbuterol, a substance on the UCI banned list. He was stripped of the titles he won at the 2010 Tour and 2012 Giro. Contador blamed the incident on an infected beef steak.

4
Contador has won the Velo d'Or, which was introduced in 1992 for the season's best cyclist, a record four times. Lance Armstrong was stripped of his five awards.

THE FACTS

Full name **Alberto Contador**

Nickname **El Pistolero**

Date of birth **December 6 1982**

Birthplace **Pinto, Madrid, Spain**

Height **5ft 9in (1.86m)**

Weight **9st 8lb (62kg)**

Discipline **All-rounder**

75

The yellow jersey

The most famous jersey in cycling is worn by the leader of the general classification after each stage of the Tour de France, but only the champion is said to 'win' it. *Statistics are for all Tours up to 2015

96

Eddy Merckx's
96 days in the jersey is more than any other rider.

8

The most number of riders to wear yellow in a single Tour is eight. It happened in 1958 and 1987.

8

Bernard Hinault
wore yellow in eight different Tours, more than any other rider. The years were 1978, 1979, 1980, 1981, 1982, 1984, 1985 and 1986.

29

Fabian Cancellara's
total of 29 days in yellow is the most of any rider without winning the Tour.

1919

The yellow jersey was introduced for the 1919 Tour, 16 years after the event's inaugural staging.

1924
Ottavio Bottecchia (Ita)

1928
Nicolas Frantz (Lux)

1935
Romain Maes (Bel)

1999
~~Lance Armstrong~~ (US)

Four riders have worn the jersey from the second stage until the last one.

* Maurice Garin (Fra) also led the Tour from the second stage until the final one of the 1903 Tour but the maillot jaune had not been introduced then.

6

Six riders have won the yellow jersey without winning a stage of the same race.

Firmin Lambot (Bel) **1922**
Roger Walkowiak (Fra) **1956**
Gastone Nencini (Ita) **1960**
Lucien Aimar (Fra) **1966**
Greg LeMond (USA) **1990**
Óscar Pereiro (Spa) **2006**

5

Five riders have won the maillot jaune the last time they entered the race

René Pottier (Fra) **1906**
Roger Lapebie (Fra) **1937**
Sylvère Maes (Bel) **1939**
Fausto Coppi (Ita) **1952**
Bradley Wiggins (GB) **2012**

10

Ten riders have won the yellow jersey the first time they entered the Tour

Maurice Garin (Fra) **1903**
Henri Cornet (Fra) **1904**
Louis Trousselier (Fra) **1905**
Jean Robic (Fra) **1947**
Fausto Coppi (Ita) **1949**
Hugo Koblet (Swi) **1951**
Jacques Anquetil (Fra) **1957**
Felice Gimondi (Ita) **1965**
Bernard Hinault (Fra) **1978**
Laurent Fignon (Fra) **1983**

Female trailblazers

Legendary female cyclists Beryl Burton, Jeannie Longo and Marianne Vos have been given full profiles elsewhere in this book, but a good number of others have served as hugely successful pioneers of the sport. Here is a selection of the most memorable.

TILLIE ANDERSON

Sweden

1875–1965

CAREER Emigrated to the United States and won all but seven of her 130 races.

MAJOR FEAT The seamstress broke the 100-mile record for women aged only 16.

LEGACY Although women began racing in 1879, for years it was seen as a novelty. Not until Anderson emerged on the scene – she was especially successful in six-day racing – was it regarded as a serious pursuit.

EILEEN SHERIDAN

Great Britain

1923–

CAREER Set national time-records at every distance from 10 to 100 miles in the 1940s and 1950s.

MAJOR FEAT Set the Land's End to John O'Groats record of 2 days 11hr 7min as a professional, sponsored by the Hercules bike firm.

LEGACY Sparked debate in national newspapers about women's physical potential and broke new ground by earning equal billing with the men whom Hercules also sponsored.

HÉLÈNE DUTRIEU

Belgium

1877–1961

CAREER Won world track titles in 1896 and 1897 and an indoor 12-day race in London in 1898.

MAJOR FEAT Set the women's first Hour Record in 1895, with a distance of 39.190km.

LEGACY For all her achievements in cycling, Dutrieu was perhaps best remembered as the fourth woman ever to be given a pilot's licence and the first to be airborne for more than an hour.

MARIANNE MARTIN

USA

1957–

CAREER Martin took up bike racing only at university and never won a national or world title, but excelled at stage racing.

MAJOR FEAT Winning the 1984 Tour Cycliste Féminin, the first ever women's version of the Tour de France.

LEGACY Her performance shattered preconceptions that women were not suited to major stage racing, especially in France, where journalists had predicted that competitors would not even finish the event.

LEONTIEN VAN MOORSEL

Netherlands

1970–

CAREER Road and track specialist who twice won the Tour Cycliste Féminin and held the Hour Record.

MAJOR FEAT Recovered from depression and anorexia nervosa to win the World Time-Trial title in 1998.

LEGACY Arguably cycling's first poster girl who wore bright lipstick and had long, painted fingernails, proving that it was possible to combine elite achievement with a glamorous image.

VICTORIA PENDLETON

Great Britain
1980–

CAREER A superstar on the track, Pendleton won a record six World Sprint titles and was twice an Olympic champion, winning the sprint race in 2008 and the keirin four years later.

LEGACY Pendleton helped to make track cycling glamorous and was the inspiration for a new generation of young female track stars in Britain. With her modelling shoots and engaging personality, as well as formidable talent and work ethic, she also played an important role in transforming track cycling from a minority pursuit to a mainstream sport during a golden era for British cycling.

YVONNE REYNDERS

Belgium
1937–

CAREER One of the most successful female riders of the 1950s and 1960s, winning four world titles in the road race and three in the individual pursuit.

MAJOR FEAT Perhaps her most remarkable achievement came in 1976 when, aged 39, she came out of retirement to win the Belgian national title and bronze in the World Road Race.

LEGACY Reynders, who used to deliver coal with her bike and trailer for a living, was a pioneer for women's cycling in the modern era. The second ever winner of the women's World Road-Race, in 1959, she helped to dispel the myth that women lacked the strength of character and physical gifts to thrive in the discipline.

ROBIN MORTON

USA
1955–

CAREER An exception to the list as Morton never actually raced, but instead got involved in the sport while following her husband on the American club racing scene.

MAJOR FEAT Remains the first and only team manager of a men's team on the UCI Tour.

LEGACY With sponsorship from Gianni Motta, Morton took her team to the 1984 Giro d'Italia and proved wrong the belief that senior management on the biggest teams should be the preserve of the men.

CAREER One of the finest road-riders of her generation, winning the Giro d'Italia Femminile and the Grande Boucle Féminine Internationale, the successor to the Tour Féminin.

MAJOR FEAT In 2008, she became the first cyclist, male or female, to win the Olympic and World Road Race in the same year.

LEGACY For all her achievements, Cooke is just as well remembered for her retirement speech in 2013, in which she excoriated the sport's powerbrokers for being prejudiced against the women's scene. She also heavily criticised the dopers who had ruined the sport's image.

NICOLE COOKE

Great Britain
1983–

1980–

Time trial legends

The time trial began in late 19th-century Britain when conventional, massed–start racing was banned on the country's roads. The race against the clock has gone on to become a key part of Grand Tours and a prestigious stand-alone event at major championships.

ON THE TOUR

For Tour de France icons such as Fausto Coppi, Jacques Anquetil and Eddy Merckx, success in its time trials was crucial to them winning the overall general classification. For specialists of the discipline such as Fabian Cancellara, it ensured temporary moments in the spotlight. This illustration depicts the stage wins of the five most successful time-triallists at the Tour and includes victories on its prologue.

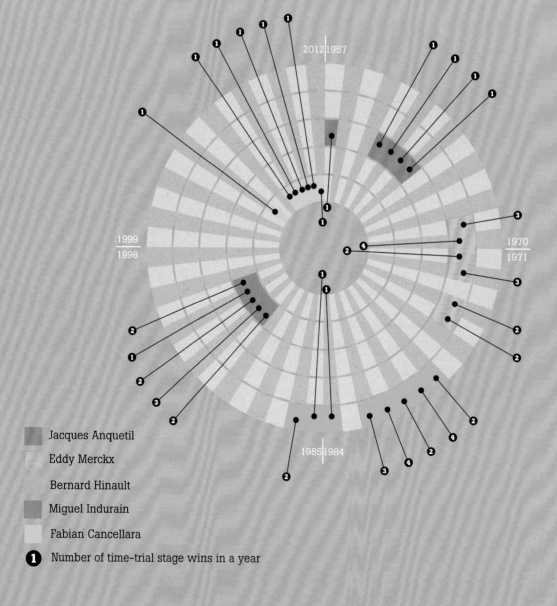

Jacques Anquetil

Eddy Merckx

Bernard Hinault

Miguel Indurain

Fabian Cancellara

1 Number of time-trial stage wins in a year

*Figures are for the years up to and including 2015

THE ULTIMATE TRIAL

The Grand Prix des Nations was the unofficial World Time-Trial Championship before the event was introduced to the Road World Championships in 1994. Staged in a variety of locations in France, the Nations first ran in 1932 over 140km but rarely exceeded 90km from 1965 until its final edition in 2004. Jacques Anquetil won it more often than any other rider, with nine victories, followed by Bernard Hinault with five wins.

AHEAD OF HER TIME

Beryl Burton dominated the women's time-trial scene in Britain, holding records over every distance from 10 miles to 100 miles. With no international scene for women in the 1950s and 1960s, she was invited to compete in the 1967 Grand Prix des Nations and finished only a minute behind the last male rider, having completed the 73km course at an average speed of 41km/h.

4

Jeannie Longo (Fra) holds the record of four women's world titles, having won in 1995, 1996, 1997 and 2001. Judith Arndt (Ger) has won the most medals in the event, with seven, including gold in 2011 and 2012. As with the men, the time trial was introduced to the women's World Championships in 1994.

4

Fabian Cancellara holds the record of four men's world titles, having won in 2006, 2007, 2009 and 2010. Tony Martin (Ger) has the second-highest tally, having triumphed in 2011, 2012 and 2013.

Wild men

Just as elite cyclists push themselves to physical extremes in the pursuit of success, so some of them have enjoyed excess away from the saddle, whether drinking, smoking or indulging in the kind of drugs that almost certainly would not have enhanced their performance.

Jacques Anquetil

After an argument over pay, the French legend spent the night before a semi-classic knocking back the spirits in the mistaken belief that the race organisers would not meet his demands, which meant Anquetil turned up at the start line severely hungover. The peloton graciously gave him a head start, only for 'Maître Jacques' to shake off the effects of the booze and win in style.

Peter Sagan

The Slovak is possibly the best all-round talent currently in the sport though he is also known for his sense of fun and love of a party. Not content with clowning around on podiums, at the Amstel Curaçao Race, he easily beat the rest of the peloton in its traditional drinking competition.

Eddy Merckx

The most successful cyclist liked to pull on the odd cigarette and was even paid to advertise them during his pomp (although some doctors at the time felt that cigarettes opened up the airways and relaxed the muscles). Quite how successful the five-time Tour de France winner would have been had he not smoked is anyone's guess.

Abdel-Kader Zaaf

As a devout Muslim, this Algerian cult-hero avoided alcohol yet inadvertently succumbed to its effects during a solo attack at the 1950 Tour. Legend has it that mischievous locals offered him a selection of alcoholic drinks in the sweltering heat, which resulted in the drunken Zaaf taking a nap under a tree. When he awoke, he set off in the opposite direction!

Bizarre prizes

Not all races reward their winners with silverware. From sweets to ancient weaponry and home appliances, champion cyclists have been furnished with some of the most unlikely spoils.

CHEESE
Tour of Britain
Stage winners on the Tour of Britain have been known to wield a wheel of local cheese above their head in celebration, as it is their reward for victory.

PIGLET
Tro Bro Leon, France
The first challenge facing competitors on this UCI 1.1 event is to survive the uncertain course as some 30 of the race's 204 kilometres are unpaved. For the winner and the first-placed Breton, the second is to work out what to do with the prize of a live piglet.

A GRIZZLY BEAR
Tour of California, USA
OK, not an actual bear, but a statue of one on a plinth. This trophy is not one for the mantelpiece, though, being about the size of a human head.

HARIBO SWEETS
Coupe de France
From 1994 to 2006, the winner of the first race in the Coupe de France was given his bodyweight in Haribo sweets as the confectioner sponsored the event. The Estonian Jaan Kirsipuu triumphed three times, which might explain why he never cut it on the mountains of the Tour de France – he withdrew from it a record 12 times.

SWORD
Toledo stage, Vuelta a España
There are never any podium arguments over the result here. Two race attendants are needed to present the winner with an enormous two-handed 'great sword'.

BEER. AND LOADS OF IT
Tour of Flanders, Belgium
In 2015, former Belgian cyclist Nico Mattan revealed that he had arranged for the winner of an intermediate sprint in Flanders to win his own bodyweight in beer. Irish rider Matt Brammeier successfully embraced the challenge and quickly became the most popular rider in the peloton.

AMBROSE THE DONKEY
Kuurne-Brussels-Kuurne Belgium
The winner of this race is presented with a cuddly ass named Ambrose. The reason? Locals from a rival town called Kuurne market-traders 'donkeys' because of their ass-pulled carts.

HUGE SAUSAGE
Tour of Austria
Enormous blocks of local cheese are a common prize at many races, but the Tour of Austria tops that with an almost body-sized sausage. Of all the prizes listed here, this one could be the wurst.

MODEL BOAT
The Tour of Qatar
Qatar organisers appeared to confuse their sports when shopping for a suitable trophy for their event when it was founded in 2002. The winner of this stage race is awarded a model sailboat.

BOWL
Tour de France
As well as prize money and the yellow jersey, the winner of the Tour also receives an elegant porcelain bowl made in a State-run factory in Sevres on the outskirts of Paris. Awarded in 'the name of the presidency of the French republic', it is one of sport's most overlooked prizes.

TRIDENT
Tirreno-Adriatico Italy
This coast-to-coast race boasts perhaps the most dramatic prize in sport. The winner receives a golden trident, the weapon associated with Neptune, the Roman god of the sea.

DAGGER
Tour of Oman
What is it with cycling and highly dangerous antiquated weaponry? The winner of Oman's showpiece event is presented with a traditional Khanjar dagger in a ceremonial case.

Vuelta a España by numbers

Key figures* drawn from the history of Spain's Grand Tour.

3,441 km

3,227km Distance of the 1935 edition, across 14 stages.
Distance of the 2016 edition, across 21 stages.

4
Joint-record holders **Laurent Jalabert** (Fra) and **Sean Kelly** (Ire) each claimed a quartet of points-jersey victories.

4,442
kilometres
Longest edition, 1941.

17
The Spaniard **Íñigo Cuesta's** record number of participations, from 1994-2010.

42.534
kilometres/hour
Winner's fastest ever average speed, set by Ángel Casero (Spa) in 2001.

2,419
kilometres
Shortest edition, 1963.

1935
First year of the race.
71
Editions of the race (up to 2016).

4
The Spaniard **Roberto Heras's** record number of overall victories, in 2000 and 2002-05.

26.262
kilometres/hour
Winner's slowest ever average speed, set by Julián Berrendero (Spain) in 1941.

14
Federico Echave (Spa) and **Cuesta** share the most number of finishes with 14. **Echave** completed every Vuelta from 1982 to 1995.

30minutes8seconds

The widest winning margin ever, which **Delio Rodríguez** set when he beat fellow Spaniard **Julián Berrendero** to win in 1945.

6seconds

The smallest winning margin – by which **Eric Caritoux** (Fra) beat **Alberto Fernández** (Spa) to triumph in 1984.

20

In 1984, Spanish legend Miguel Indurain became the youngest ever rider to lead the Vuelta at the age of 20.

207

Most number of participants, 2002.

32

Least number of participants, 1941.

1,092,050euros

Total prize pool

39

Delio Rodríguez's record number of stage victories. The Spaniard won them all in the 1940s.

13

Freddy Maertens (Bel) set this record for stage victories in one edition in 1977.

58

Alex Zülle (Swi) twice a winner and twice runner-up, spent an unsurpassed 58 days leading the race.

5

José Luis Laguía (Spa) won five mountains classification in the 1980s, more than any rider in history.

*Figures correct up to 2016.

ICON Bernard Hinault

Though undeniably an all-time great, Bernard Hinault's, palmares does not include as many victories as other icons of the sport profiled in this book, but then the Frenchman would almost certainly have won more titles had he not suffered from a chronic knee problem. As it is, his record makes awesome reading, including as it does multiple victories in each Grand Tour and a clutch of prestigious one-day wins. For all his talent, however, Hinault was known almost as much for his tenacity and single-mindedness that led to almost as many run-ins with the authorities and rivals as it did bitterly fought victories.

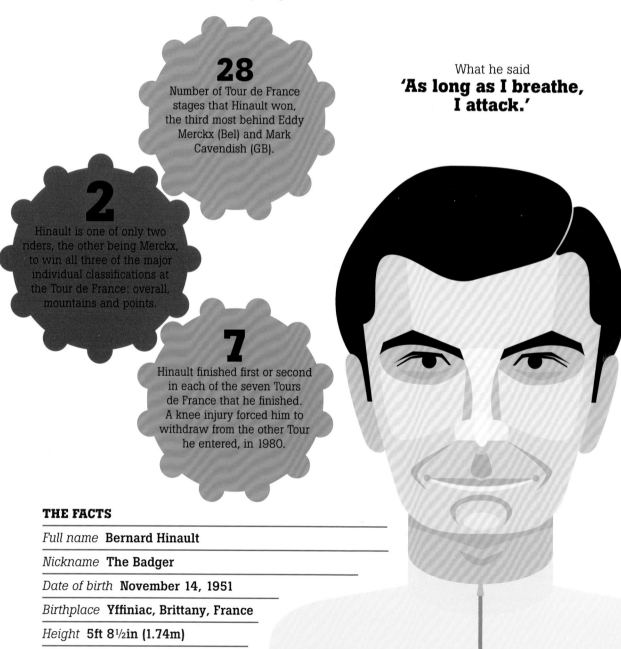

28
Number of Tour de France stages that Hinault won, the third most behind Eddy Merckx (Bel) and Mark Cavendish (GB).

2
Hinault is one of only two riders, the other being Merckx, to win all three of the major individual classifications at the Tour de France: overall, mountains and points.

7
Hinault finished first or second in each of the seven Tours de France that he finished. A knee injury forced him to withdraw from the other Tour he entered, in 1980.

What he said
'As long as I breathe, I attack.'

THE FACTS

Full name **Bernard Hinault**

Nickname **The Badger**

Date of birth **November 14, 1951**

Birthplace **Yffiniac, Brittany, France**

Height **5ft 8½in (1.74m)**

THE TEAMS

1975-77
Gitane-Campagnolo

1978-1983
Renault-Elf-Gitane

1984-1986
La Vie Claire

THE MAJOR VICTORIES

Other
5 Grand Prix des Nations
One-day races and Classics
1 Amstel Gold Race
1 Gent-Wevelgem
3 La Flèche Wallonne
1 Paris-Roubaix
3 Tour of Lombardy
2 Liège-Bastogne-Liège
1 Word Road Race
Stage races
1 Tour de Romandie
3 Critérium du Dauphiné Libéré
Grand Tours
2 Vuelta a España
3 Giro d'Italia
5 Tour de France

15

Probably Hinault's most memorable one-day victory was at the 1980 World Road Race on one of the event's toughest ever courses, comprising 20 laps of the Domency climb in the French Alps. Not only did Hinault win by more than a minute, but he was also one of only 15 riders to finish of the 107 who started.

ANIMAL INSTINCT
Hinault was nicknamed Le Blaireau or The Badger. Some said it was because, he wore a hairband that made him look like the animal, but Hinault claimed it was a term of affection among local cyclists in his youth. Tactically, it suited him because he was never more dangerous than when cornered.

The individual sprint

The blue-riband event of track cycling, the individual sprint is arguably also the most dramatic, rewarding only those riders who combine fierce explosive power, a subtle tactical mind and nerves of steel.

Finish line

3

Only three men have twice won the Olympic title:
Daniel Morelon
(Fra) 1968, 1972
Jens Fiedler
(Ger) 1992, 1996
Jason Kenny
(GB) 2012, 2016

THE HISTORY

● The men's individual sprint has been included at every World Championships since the first one in 1893. There was a version for amateurs until 1993. The professional race has been running since 1895. There has been a women's race in all but two Championships (1988 and 1992) since it was introduced in 1958.
● The discipline has been part of every Olympics except two: the 1904 St Louis Games and Stockholm 1912. There has been a women's race in each Games since they were first admitted to Olympic track cycling in 1988.

1

One woman has managed it:
Félicia Ballanger
(Fra) 1996, 2000

THE TACTICS

The 'second' ❷ has an important tactical advantage because they get to travel in the opponent's **slipstream**. The lead-out rider ❶ will occasionally try to catch their rival off-guard with an early attack aimed at building an unassailable lead, but usually the pair will set off at a **snail's pace** and maintain it for the first lap.

10

Koichi Nakano holds the record of 10 men's world titles, having won it every year between 1977 and 1986.

6

Three women share the record of six world titles:
Galina Yermolayeva (USSR) 1958, 1959, 1960, 1961, 1962, 1972
Galina Tsareva (USSR) 1969, 1970, 1971, 1977, 1978, 1979
Victoria Pendleton (GB) 2005, 2007, 2008, 2009, 2010, 2012

THE RULES

● In official competition, competitors are subject to a qualifying round in which they are timed over a flying lap, with the fastest riders going through to the knockout stage. There are also repechage races in which losing riders get another change to progress.

● In official UCI events, the knockout stage consists of two-man races over three laps of the track.

● The winner is decided in one race until the quarter-finals and then on a best-of-three format, with the 'lead-out' rider for the first race decided by drawing lots. He must lead for all of the first lap.

Black line

Sprinter's line

Stayer's line

Cat-and-mouse baiting ensues in which one rider attempts to goad the other into making the first move. This can result in track-stands in which the riders remain in one position, edging back and forth to keep balanced, albeit within a set time limit.

Riders will usually launch their **attack** at some point in the final 200m as it is extremely difficult to hold top speed for any longer. Once the sprint is initiated, riders are not allowed to cross the red sprinter's line that runs 85cm from inside of the track.

The rise and fall of Marco Pantani

Few riders have suffered such a dramatic decline in fortunes as Marco Pantani, the adored Italian rider whose form and private life fell apart as he became dogged by doping allegations and battled with substance abuse.

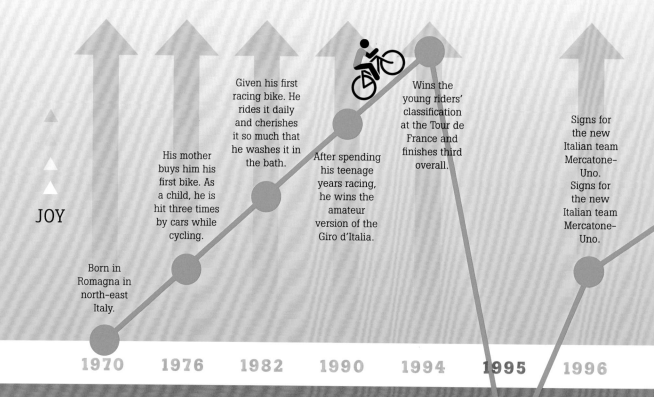

JOY

Given his first racing bike. He rides it daily and cherishes it so much that he washes it in the bath.

His mother buys him his first bike. As a child, he is hit three times by cars while cycling.

Wins the young riders' classification at the Tour de France and finishes third overall.

After spending his teenage years racing, he wins the amateur version of the Giro d'Italia.

Signs for the new Italian team Mercatone-Uno.
Signs for the new Italian team Mercatone-Uno.

Born in Romagna in north-east Italy.

1970   **1976**   **1982**   **1990**   **1994**   **1995**   **1996**

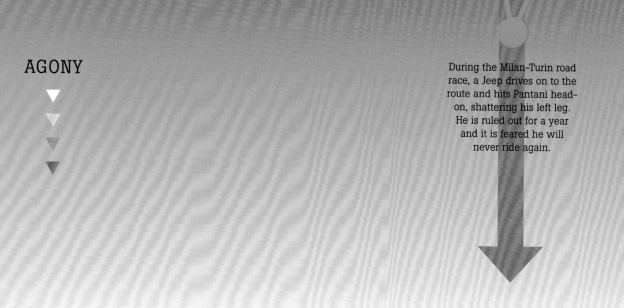

AGONY

During the Milan-Turin road race, a Jeep drives on to the route and hits Pantani head-on, shattering his left leg. He is ruled out for a year and it is feared he will never ride again.

Wins the Giro- Tour double. His victory helps to salvage the Tour's reputation after it was blighted by the doping scandal surrounding the Festina Affair.

Returns to action at the Tour and sets the record for the fastest ascent of Alpe d'Huez.

After a self-enforced year out, he returns to racing and beats Lance Armstrong in a memorable battle in the Alps after the Texan called him Elefantino because of his bald head and large ears. Armstrong, who bonked during the stage, would later call it his worst ever day on the bike.

1997   1998   **1999**   2000   **2001**   2003   2004

Tells a journalist that he is 'done with cycling forever' after several failed attempts to quit his drug habit in rehab, including one at a clinic in Cuba recommended to him by the footballer Diego Maradona, himself an addict.

Fails a haematocrit blood test while leading the Giro and is thrown out of the race with one mountain stage left.

Pantani is banned from racing after police find a syringe with traces of insulin in his room during the Giro. His personal life has spiralled and he is now on anti-depressants and struggling with a cocaine addiction.

Pantani is found dead in a hotel in the Italian seaside resort of Rimini, having suffered a cerebral edema and heart failure as a result of acute cocaine poisoning. Twenty thousand mourners attend his funeral.

Monument #2
Tour of Flanders

De Ronde – 'The Tour'
First edition: 1913
Distance: 255km (2016)
Route (since 2012); Bruges-Oudenaarde

The showpiece event of the several tough races that take place in the cycling-mad region of Flanders during late March and early April, De Ronde was established to revive the sport at a time when it was in decline in Belgium. It has lasted to become not only one of the toughest one-day events on the calendar but also a focal point for Flemish identity, with thousands of the region's flags distributed on race day and locally bred winners earning a lasting place in Flanders folklore. One of the two cobbled Classics along with Paris-Roubaix, its route is best known for the short, sharp and often precipitously steep climbs.

The Flemish flag

The Flemish flag is a defining feature of the race, with giant standards hung over the finishing straight. The best riders in each generation of the race are named the Lion of Flanders after its famous emblem.

BRUGES

BRUGES

BELGIUM

OUDENAARDE

Koppenberg

Taaienberg

YPRES

KORTRUK

Oude-Kwaremont

Paterberg

Km

0   20   40   60   80   100   120

1969: The greatest victory

By this period in Eddy Merckx's career, he started favourite in every road race that he entered, but the Tour of Flanders still eluded him, prompting the Belgian press to claim he lacked the all-round qualities to win it. In 1969, fired up by the criticism and aware that the rest of the peloton was likely to collude against him, Merckx embarked on a devastating solo attack halfway through the race that eventually earnt him the largest winning margin in the history of the race: 5min 36sec.

Most victories

Six riders have won the race three times.

Achille Buysse (Bel)
1940, 1941, 1943
Fiorenzo Magni (Ita)
1949-1951
Eric Leman (Bel)
1970, 1972, 1973
Johan Museeuw (Bel)
1993, 1995, 1998
Tom Boonen (Bel)
2005, 2006, 2012
Fabian Cancellara (Swi)
2010, 2013, 2014

The forgotten founder

Not until the race was 100 years old did historians discover that the principal force behind the creation of the race was a Belgian cycling journalist called Leon van den Haute. While previously his colleague Karel Van Wijnendaele had been credited with its formation, in 2013, Belgian academics found that Van den Haute conceived the idea, organised its finances, set the route and even laid out the road markings.

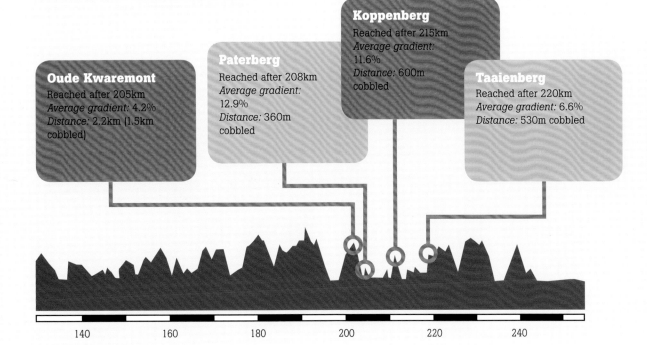

Koppenberg
Reached after 215km
Average gradient: 11.6%
Distance: 600m cobbled

Paterberg
Reached after 208km
Average gradient: 12.9%
Distance: 360m cobbled

Oude Kwaremont
Reached after 205km
Average gradient: 4.2%
Distance: 2.2km (1.5km cobbled)

Taaienberg
Reached after 220km
Average gradient: 6.6%
Distance: 530m cobbled

140   160   180   200   220   240

Design icons

From the road bike designed by Damien Hirst to the track bike built with spare parts from a washing machine, these are six of the most memorable designs in the history of the sport.

Coppi's 1952 Bianchi

The bike on which Fausto Coppi rode to his second Tour de France victory is one of the most iconic in the sport. Aficionados like its famous Bianchi Celeste, but it was innovative too, being one of the first bikes with a double chainset and a cable-operated, parallelogram-shaped derailleur, both of which became standard. Previously, the gears on most racing bikes were changed with stick-like levers and either a quick-release mechanism or a less efficient, rear derailleur.

Boardman's Lotus 108

Though Graeme Obree innovated the aerodynamic 'Superman' position in which the rider's arms were extended out in front, Chris Boardman's Lotus 108 is the most famous design to adopt it. Boardman helped to develop the bike himself and won the individual pursuit on it at the 1992 Olympics, Great Britain's first cycling gold at the Games in 72 years. The UCI later banned the riding position.

Armstrong's 'Butterfly' Trek Madone

Lance Armstrong persuaded seven of his favourite artists to decorate his frames with a view to raising money for his LiveStrong charity. Used on the final stage of the 2009 Tour de France, Damien Hirst's design sparked controversy because the Briton used real butterflies to adorn the frame and rims. The bike was later auctioned for $500,000 at Sotheby's.

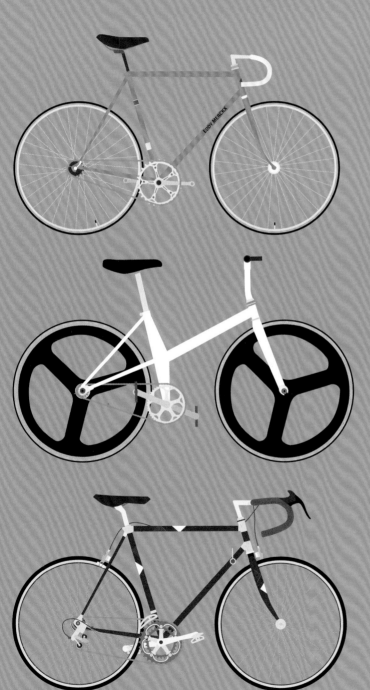

Merckx's hour-record Colnago

When asked as a young man to outline his professional ambitions, Eddy Merckx replied: 'To win the Tour de France and set a new hour record.' The great Belgian realised the first ambition five times, and managed the second one in 1972 on a bike built in collaboration with the celebrated frame-builder Ernesto Colnago. It was among the lightest and most innovative designs of its time.

Obree's Old Faithful

The Scotsman Graeme Obree discarded all conventional design to build a bike for his successful assault on the Hour Record in 1993. Inspired by downhill skiers, his handlebars tucked his arms into his side, while the down tube and top tube were replaced with a main 'beam' that put his knees closer together. Famously, he used discarded BMX tubes and bearings salvaged from a washing machine.

LeMond's Look G86

Greg LeMond signalled a step-change in bike design when he became the first rider to win the Tour de France on a carbon frame when riding the Look G86 in 1986. His La Vie Claire team-mate Bernard Hinault finished second on the same model, with only three minutes separating the men at the end of a compelling Tour.

Tragic heroes

Tom Simpson's death during the 1967 Tour de France (see 'Cycling's greatest tragedy') is not the only fatality to have blighted cycling. Here is a selection of other great talents who died in their prime.

Age

28

RENÉ POTTIER
Born 1879 **Died** 1907
France

Career A climbing specialist whose career peaked with his victory at the 1906 Tour de France. He also twice finished on the podium at Paris-Roubaix.

Tragedy Pottier hanged himself in the January after his Tour win, having discovered that his wife had found a lover while he was competing in the race. A memorial to him was erected at Ballon d'Alsace, the site of his decisive attack during the 1906 Tour, which a contemporary report described as pushing back 'the boundaries of the possible'.

33

OTTAVIO BOTTECCHIA
Born 1894 **Died** 1927
Italy

Career The first Italian winner of the Tour de France, claiming the title in both 1924 and 1925. He also finished second in 1923 and won nine Tour stages in total.

Tragedy The then recently-retired Bottecchia was found dead on a lonely country road near his home in Veneto, with his skull smashed and other bones broken. The cause of death was never established, but theories included an assassination by fascists unhappy with his liberal leanings, a Mafioso hit and an attack from a farmer who caught Bottecchia eating his grapes.

36

STAN OCKERS
Born 1920 **Died** 1956
Belgium

Career A superb all-rounder who twice won the points' classification on the Tour and twice finished second overall in the race. He was also only the second rider ever to complete the 'Ardennes double' by winning the La Flèche Wallonne and Liège-Bastogne-Liège classics in the same season.

Tragedy Died as a result of head injuries he suffered in a crash during a track race in Antwerp. This was only a year after the Belgian won the World Road Race title, contributing to the superstition that the rainbow jersey was cursed.

28

SERSE COPPI
Born 1923 **Died** 1951
Italy

Career The younger brother of the great Fausto Coppi rode in support of his sibling on the Bianchi team but was a strong rider in his own right. The highlight of his career was to be declared the joint winner of the 1949 Paris-Roubaix.

Tragedy Serse died from head injuries that he suffered when he crashed in the final sprint of the Giro del Piemonte semi-classic after his wheel got caught in tramlines. His injuries did not initially appear serious and he rode to his hotel but his condition then quickly deteriorated. He died in his brother's arms in hospital.

23

KNUD JENSEN
Born 1936 **Died** 1960
Denmark

Career Jensen's star was still in the ascendancy when he died aged only 23 and he surely would have won much more. However, he had by then been an individual champion at the Nordic track championships.

Tragedy Jensen wanted to pull out of the team time trial at the Olympics because he felt dizzy in the saddle but his teammates persuaded him to go on as they were a man down. In searing 40C heat, he passed out in the saddle, fractured his skull in the crash and died in hospital. The official cause of death was given as sunstroke but amphetamine was found in his system.

22

JEAN-PIERRE MONSERÉ
Born 1948 **Died** 1971
Belgium

Career Monseré was a highly promising rider who won the Tour of Lombardy aged only 21 and became the second-youngest ever winner of the World Road Race title at the same age. The Belgian Karel Kaers is the youngest.

Tragedy The Belgian died during the Grote Jaarmarktprijs road race after he collided with a car that had driven on to the course. In a cruel twist of fate, Monseré's seven-year-old son died in a collision with a car while riding his racing bike five years later. Freddy Maertens, the Belgian two-time world champion, had given the boy the bike as a gift.

34

MARCO PANTANI
Born 1970 **Died** 2004
Italy

Career One of the finest climbers of all time, Pantani won the Tour-Giro d'Italia double in 1998, eight stages in each of those two races and the Tour's mountains classification.

Tragedy Pantani was found dead in a hotel room in Rimini, having suffered a cerebral edema and heart failure as the result of acute cocaine poisoning – he had been supplied with an ultra-pure form of the drug. His girlfriend later revealed that Pantani had started using cocaine after he was thrown out of the 1999 Giro for doping.

24

FABIO CASARTELLI
Born 1970 **Died** 1995
Italy

Career A sadly short career peaked with his victory in the 1993 Olympic road race. He had time to compete in only one Grand Tour, finishing 107th in the 1993 Giro.

Tragedy On stage 15 of the 1995 Tour, Casartelli crashed on the descent of the Col de Portet d'Aspet. His head struck concrete blocks beside the road and he was declared dead while being flown to hospital. It was asserted that his injuries would have been less severe had he been wearing a helmet but they were still not made compulsory until 2003.

The modern road and track bikes

Designers produce road and track bikes for professional teams by spending hundreds of hours on wind-tunnel analysis, stress-testing and computer simulation. In the case of both bikes, the result is a model of aerodynamic engineering.

Road bike

1 Helmet
The tragic death of Andrei Kivilev from head injuries in 2003 led the UCI to make helmets compulsory. They had tried once before, in 1991, but a cyclists' protest blocked the ruling.

2 Frame
Made from carbon fibre, making it both strong and lightweight. Typical weight is 1.5kg.

3 Gears
Electronic gear shifters and the brake levers are integrated into one unit and placed beneath the handlebar 'hoods', ensuring they can be pressed easily in different positions on the bike.

4 Brakes
Carbon clinchers and carbon rims. The peloton was using hydraulic disc brakes in 2016 but the UCI suspended them after the Spaniard Francisco Ventoso was injured by them in a crash Paris-Roubaix.

5 Saddles
A combination of plastic and carbon fibre, encased in a leather shell. Each rider has a slightly different type of saddle, in a slightly different position.

6 Drivetrain
Oval-shaped chainrings to boost efficiency, with a longer-diameter gearing during the downstroke because most power is generated then.

7 Wheels
The perfect wheel is aerodynamic, light and stiff, to ensure no energy is lost through flex. Generally, carbon-fibre wheels with deep-section, 50mm rims are the most popular. Their toroidal profile increases the efficiency of the air flow around them, which is especially important in crosswinds. Deeper rims are used on time trials and shallower ones in the mountains.

8 Tyres
Tubular tyres glued to rims: the lightest possible type. Professional teams tend to use 25mm-wide tyres in road races, increasing to 30mm for cobbled surfaces, to improve suspension and traction.

9 Forks
Steep to make the steering more responsive.

10 6.8kg
UCI's minimum weight for all track bikes

Track bike

1 Seat tube
While the seat tube on a road bike will tend to be set at less than 74 degrees, on a track bike it will be at angled just over that figure, to assist more aggressive riding.

2 Rear wheel
Full disc wheel to improve aerodynamics. Constructed from carbon fibre, no freewheel mechanism.

3 Bottom bracket
High position to ensure the pedals do not touch the steeply banked track.

4 Gearing
One chainwheel and one sprocket. As it is fixed gear, the size ratio is very important. A lower gear ratio allows quicker acceleration, while a larger gear ratio is better for sustaining a high speed.

5 Dropouts
Horizontal dropouts to enable the rider to adjust the chain tension by moving the wheel slightly forward or backward – which, in turn, affects the efficiency with which the rider transfers power.

6 Frame
Constructed from carbon fibre, making it light but stiff. Track bikes use slightly thicker carbon than road bikes to withstand the extreme power applied to them. Typical weight is 1.4kg.

7 No brakes
Brakes are unnecessary because the direction of travel is uniform, there are no corners and no rider can stop quicker than another. To slow down, the rider pushes the cranks backwards.

8 Tyres
Very slick tyres: 19-20mm width, made from soft rubber and pumped to a high pressure of more than 120psi. Indoor track tyres do not require any tread, while new tyres are rubbed with white vinegar to remove any lacquer left from the manufacturing process.

9 Forks
Steep to make the steering more responsive.

10 6.8kg
UCI's minimum weight for all track bikes

ICON Miguel Indurain

Time-triallist par excellence, awesome physical specimen and quietly precise tactician, Miguel 'Big Mig' Indurain dominated the Tour de France during the first half of the 1990s with almost tyrannical consistency. In an era when Tour time trials were much longer than today, his tactic was to establish a lead on them and then do whatever it took in the mountains to sustain it. Combined with his introverted personality, such an approach did not make for the most compelling viewing but it was brutally effective. As a result, this modest son of Pamplona jointly holds the record for Tour victories and is one of only six riders to achieve the Tour-Giro double in the same season, a feat he managed in successive seasons.

52.4km/h
Indurain's average speed when he won the 64km individual time trial at the 1992 Tour de France. It was the fastest of his ten time-trial victories on the Tour.

'Indurain will enter the record books as someone who never took risks.'
Eddy Merckx

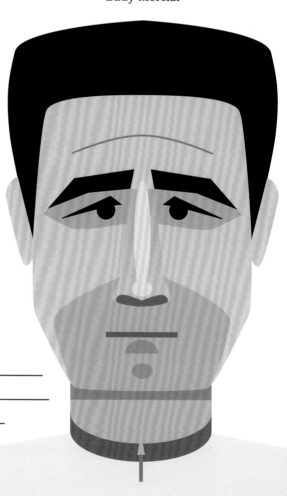

$8,000,000
Indurain retired suddenly in 1995 despite claiming that he was in strong enough shape to win a sixth consecutive Tour. The decision was reportedly prompted by him being unable to find a team willing to pay him a $8million salary.

THE FACTS

Full name **Miguel Indurain Larraya**

Nickname **Big Mig**

Born **July 16, 1964**

Date of birth **Villava, Navarre, Spain**

Height **6ft 2in (1.88m)**

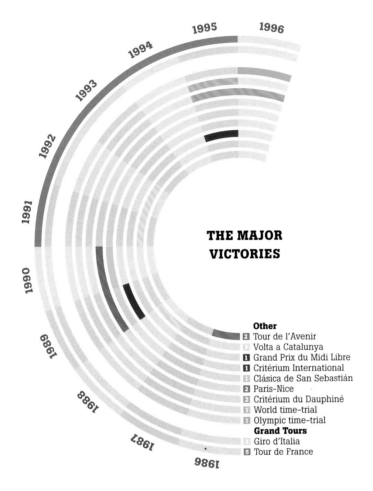

THE MAJOR VICTORIES

1996
1995
1994
1993
1992
1991
1990
1989
1988
1987
1986

Other
2 Tour de l'Avenir
3 Volta a Catalunya
1 Grand Prix du Midi Libre
1 Critérium International
1 Clásica de San Sebastián
2 Paris-Nice
2 Critérium du Dauphiné
1 World time-trial
1 Olympic time-trial
Grand Tours
2 Giro d'Italia
5 Tour de France

What he said
'The way I rode is the way I am. Ultimately when you are out on the road that is also the way you are with other people. Some say I could have been more aggressive and got more victories, but if you don't behave the way you are, you don't feel comfortable with yourself.'

THE TEAMS

1984–89
Reynolds

1990–1997
Banesto

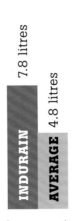

28 beats per minute / 72 beats per minute — Resting heart rate

7.8 litres / 4.8 litres — Lung capacity

50 litres / 50 litres — Cardiac output

INDURAIN / AVERAGE

INDURAIN – THE STATS
Average v Fit male cyclist

Staff of the modern road team

The senior cyclists attract nearly all of the attention but there is a significant amount of support staff in any team, as well as ranks of junior competitors. Lotto-Soudal released these figures in 2016.

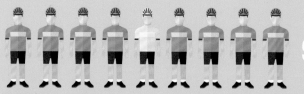

9

Grand Tour squad
Includes one leader, with the remaining riders – the domestiques - supporting him.

27

Men's pro squad
Other members of the squad compete at races across the calendar.

24

Men's under-23 squad
Compete in junior races in the hope of building enough experience to break into the pro squad.

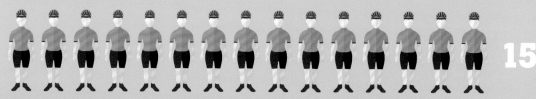

15

Women's pro squad
Lotto-Soudal also have a women's team, with a squad of 15. Despite a vast difference in prize money for the sexes, cycling is one of the fastest growing women's sports.

Medical staff
Doctors, physiotherapists, a mental-health professional and nurse.

Mechanics
Maintain all of the team's equipment.

Commercial department
Responsible for the administration of revenue and expenses.

Management and admin
The top dogs, in charge of a team's commitments, sponsors and general direction, amongst many other duties.

Bus drivers
Full-time drivers of the team's other means of transportation.

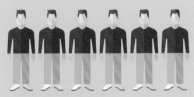

Directeur sportifs
The 'team managers' who dictate strategy during a race.

Soigneurs
'One who cares for others.' Responsible for advising, massaging and escorting the rider. An encyclopaedic knowledge of cycling is a must.

Naming rights

The finest cyclists have earnt some memorable nicknames. Here is a collection of the best.

THE HERON

Fausto Coppi was named after the waterbird partly because he appeared almost to fly across mountains but also as he had a beak-like nose, barrel chest and long, spindly calves. More flattering was his other nickname, *il Campionissimo*, or Champion of Champions, a title bestowed only on very best Italians riders. Costante Girardengo and Alfredo Binda were the other two men accorded the honour.

THE OLD MAN

(Il Vecchio)

Coppi's arch rival, Gino Bartali, was as tough as they come. He won the Tour de France in 1938 and, after World War II had robbed him of what should have been his prime years, returned to the Tour a full 10 years later to triumph again as a veteran – hence his nickname.

THE EMPEROR OF HERENTALS

Also known as 'The King of the Classics', Rik Van Looy was a hard-as-nails Flamand and the first rider to win all five Monuments, a feat since achieved by Roger De Vlaeminck and Eddy Merckx. Van Looy won 379 road races, including 37 Grand Tour stages.

THE CANNIBAL

Though it sounds unlikely, this nickname was coined after Eddy Merckx's French team-mate Christian Raymond told his young daughter that the Belgian's insatiable hunger for victories meant that he never let anyone else win. She christened him the Cannibal and it stuck.

THE LION KING

Also known as 'Super Mario' or simply 'Cipo', Italy's Mario Cipollini was a giant in build and in personality. By far the fastest road sprinter of his era, he won 191 races but is most remembered for the often outrageous designs of his racing strip, which made him one of cycling's great pin-ups.

THE PIRATE

Fans loved Marco Pantani for his aggressive climbing style, but the fact that the Italian looked like ocean-going rebel helped, too: the 1998 Tour champion shaved his head, wore a pair of hooped gold ear-rings and donned a bandana to keep sweat from his eyes.

THE HOBGOBLIN OF THE BRITTANY MOOR

At 5ft 3in, Jean Robic owed his nickname to his elfin-like appearance and his place of birth. The winner of the 1947 Tour's other epithets were scarcely more complimentary: Kid Goat, partly because of the Frenchman's climbing ability, and Leather Head, as he always wore a crash helmet after fracturing his skull in 1944.

THE PEDALLER OF CHARM

One of the most elegant and stylish riders of all time, Swiss ace Hugo Koblet took out a comb and dabbed his face with eau de cologne as he approached the line at the end of his epic lone breakaway triumphs. The first non-Italian to win the Giro, in 1950, a year later he triumphed in the Tour with virtually no team support.

THE EAGLE OF TOLEDO

Federico Bahamontes was named after the bird of prey because of the way he soared, apparently effortlessly, through the mountains - most memorably when he dominated and won the 1959 Tour in the era of great climbers. But while the classy Spaniard left opposition for dead when racing over the peaks, he was a timid descender and would be swept up once the road levelled out.

THE ANGEL OF THE MOUNTAINS

Diminutive in build, the baby-faced Charly Gaul romped away from the field on the toughest climbs, spinning impossibly low gears and excelling whenever the weather turned nasty, as on an epic stage through the Chartreuse that set the seal on the Luxembourger's 1958 Tour victory.

THE YO-YO

Jan Ullrich was given one of the sport's crueller nicknames because the 1997 Tour winner allowed his weight to yo-yo. The German would balloon in the close season but then get in reasonable shape for the summer through an intense calorie-cutting programme.

SPARTACUS

Fabian Cancellara was named after the heroic Thracian gladiator because the Swiss rider thrived when race conditions were most difficult. The winner of seven Classics, among other titles, he had the sobriquet emblazoned on his bike before retiring in 2016 after a phenomenal 16-year career.

THE TANK CAR

At less than 12st yet 6ft tall, Tony Martin's physique hardly suggests an armoured military vehicle. But the nickname Der Panzerwagen suits him because of the fearsome combination of speed and power that enabled him to excel at the time trial, winning his fourth individual world title in 2016.

THE SHARK

From the Heron to the Seagull (Johann Museeuw) to the Butterfly of Maastricht (Tom Domoulin), cyclists have often been compared to animals. Italy's Vincenzo Nibali is called the Shark of Messina because by the time you see him making an attack, it is already too late to respond.

The keirin

The keirin is a motor-paced track event in which riders usually follow a derny, a small motorised bike. The race lasts about 2km – eight laps of an Olympic track – with the derny driver starting relatively slowly and gradually increasing speed until about 600m from the end, at which point the driver pulls off the track, leaving the riders to fight out a hectic sprint for the line. It is a spectacular discipline that requires a high turn of speed allied to tactical nous and heaps of courage.

BIG IN JAPAN

● The keirin originated in Japan, where it emerged as a gambling-driven sport in 1948. It remains popular there, with the equivalent of about £100million bet on it annually at some 47 purpose-built velodromes across the country. It is one of only five sports that can be legally gambled on in Japan, along with motor cycling, horse racing, powerboats and football.

● The top riders in Japan – and some from abroad who want to profit from the lucrative appearance fees - attend a monastery-like keirin school, where they are expected to train and study for 15 hours a day.

● To make it easier to bet on races, riders wear one of nine standard colours and are known only by a number. Much like with horse-racing form guides, gamblers are given information on riders that includes past results, blood group, thigh size and – this is not a joke – star sign.

● Only one Japanese rider has won the world title, Harumi Honda in 1987, and none has triumphed at the Olympics. That is because top riders prefer to stay at home where they can earn more competing on the domestic keirin scene than by riding abroad. The most successful competitors in Japan each rake in around £1.5million a year.

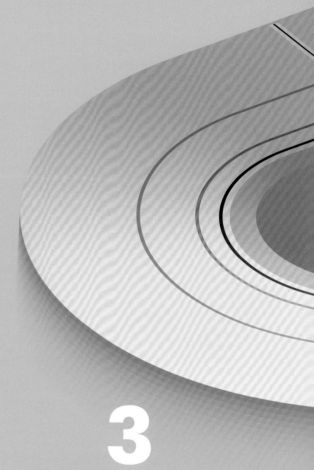

3

Michael Hübner (Ger) and **Sir Chris Hoy** (GB) share the record for the most men's world titles, with three apiece. **Hübner** won in 1990, 1991 and 1992, before **Hoy** triumphed in 2007, 2008 and 2012. **Hoy** is also the only man to have twice won the Olympic title, in 2008 and 2012.

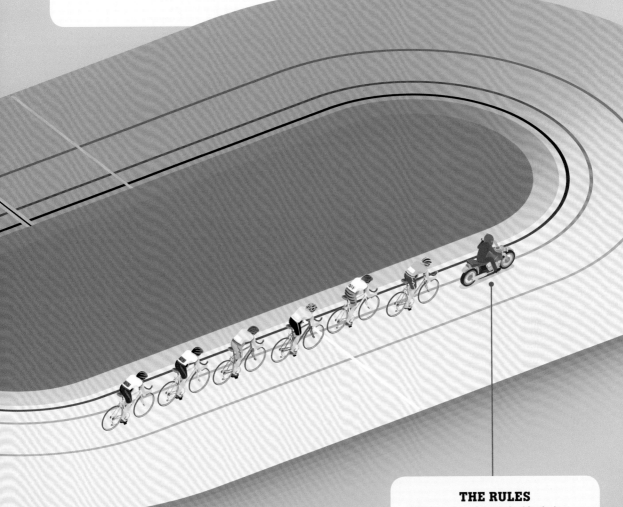

3

Australia's **Anna Meares** has won the most women's world titles, claiming gold in 2011, 2012 and 2015.

THE RULES
- Riders draw lots to decide their position on the start line.
- The pacer is limited to a top speed of 50km/h for men and 45km/h for women.
- At the Olympics, 12 riders qualify for the second round through a series of heats. The top six then contest the final, with the bottom six competing in another race to decide 7th–12th places.

Sprint kings

The task of comparing riders from different eras is especially hard, and this sprinters' top 10 is a strictly personal choice, but no one would argue that the names on it, placed in chronological order, did not possess formidable finishing kicks. *Figures correct up to and including the 2015 season.

RIK VAN STEENBERGEN
Belgium
Professional career:
1943–1966

- 4
- 42
- 6

ANDRÉ DARRIGADE
France
Professional career:
1951–1966

- 1959, 1961
- 22
- 1

RIK VAN LOOY
Belgium
Professional career:
1953–1970

- 1963
- 7
- 12
- 1959, 1965
- 18

EDDY MERCKX
Belgium
Professional career:
1965–1978

- 1969, 1971, 1972
- 34
- **1968, 1973**
- 34
- 1973
- 6

FREDDY MAERTENS
Belgium
Professional career:
1973–1987

- 1976, 1978, 1981
- 16
- 2077
- 13

Memorable victory
Van Steenbergen won the World Road Race title three times, a feat that no rider has bettered. Perhaps his most compelling victory, though, was in the 1952 Paris–Roubaix when Fausto Coppi repeatedly, but unsuccessfully, tried to shake him off, and the brilliant Belgian eventually won with his signature sprint.

Memorable victory
Darrigade was renowned for launching his finishing kick earlier than many specialist sprinters, as if challenging rivals into trying to overtake him. Most impressive among his best victories came in the 1959 World Road Race when he beat Michele Gismondi (Ita) and Noël Foré (Bel) into second and third respectively.

Memorable victory
So confident was he of winning the first of his consecutive World Road Race titles, 'The Emperor of Herentals' turned up at the East German venue for the 1960 event with a supply of neatly folded rainbow jerseys already stashed in his suitcase. A year later, he won again with the spokes on his back wheel coming loose as a result of the sheer strength of his finishing sprint.

Memorable victory
Merckx won the first of his three World Road Race titles in 1967 by beating the brilliant former champion Jan Janssen (Ned) by half a bike-length in a thrilling sprint finish in Heerlen, Holland, after almost seven hours out on the road.

Memorable victory
Maertens won his first World Road Race title at the peak of his career in 1976 but, by the time of the 1981 edition, no one expected him to claim a second title because he had gone three years without a significant victory. In fact, he rediscovered his superb form of old and beat Giuseppe Saronni (Ita) in a thrilling climax.

■ Tour de France points jersey
■ Tour de France individual stage wins
■ Giro d'Italia points jersey
■ Giro d'Italia individual stage wins
■ Vuelta a España points jersey
■ Vuelta a España individual stage wins

SEAN KELLY
Ireland
Professional career:
1977–1994

■ 1982, 1983, 1985, 1989
■ 5
■ 1980, 1985, 1986, 1988
■ 16

MARIO CIPOLLINI
Italy
Professional career:
1989–2008

■ 12
■ **1992, 1997, 2002**
■ 42
■ 3

DJAMOLIDINE ABDOUJAPAROV
Uzbekistan
Professional career:
1990–1997

■ 1991, 1993, 1994
■ **1994**
■ 1992

ERIK ZABEL
Germany
Professional career:
1993–2005

■ 1996, 1997, 1998, 1999, 2000, 2001
■ 12
■ 2002, 2003, 2004
■ 8

MARK CAVENDISH
Great Britain
Professional career:
2005–

■ 2011
■ 26
■ **2013**
■ 15
■ 2010
■ 3

Memorable victory
Like Merckx, Kelly was known as an all-rounder, but he was a superb sprinter nonetheless and won the 1983 Tour of Lombardy by half a wheel after a breathtaking five-man surge for the line involving four of the biggest names in the peloton: Francesco Moser (Ita), Greg LeMond (USA), Adri van der Poel (Ned) and Hennie Kuiper (Ned).

Memorable victory
As winner of the most stages of the Giro, with 42, it is difficult to pick only one victory for the flamboyant 'Super Mario', but the 42nd was pretty special as he edged out Robbie McEwen, the Australian who was among his closest rivals, by mere centimetres in 2003. In so doing, he broke a record that Alfredo Binda (Ita) had set 70 years earlier.

Memorable victory
Not so much a win as an achievement. In 1991, when he needed only to finish the final stage of the Tour to win the green jersey, 'The Tashkent Terror' crashed into road barriers and was sent somersaulting through the air but still managed to get back on his bike to ride the final metres, albeit with medical staff walking beside him.

Memorable victory
The German has more than 200 victories to his name. Few would have tasted sweeter than his victory over Stuart O'Grady on the penultimate day of the 2001 Tour. The Australian had led Zabel on the points classification for half the race but the result meant he won the green jersey for the sixth year in succession.

Memorable victory
The Tour's most successful specialist sprinter – and arguably the greatest of all – the 'Manx Missile' has had many memorable wins but none were more thrilling than his one triumph at the 2009 Milan-San Remo where he survived over the tough, hilly course and closed a 10-metre gap to Germany's Heinrich Haussler over the final 100 metres.

ICON **Laurent Fignon**

The supremely gifted Fignon made his name by winning the Tour de France the first two times he entered it, an unsurpassed feat, yet he is just as strongly associated with perhaps the Tour's most gallant defeat. In 1989, he was leading the race going into the final-stage time trial only for Greg LeMond to overtake him on the general classification and win by eight seconds, the narrowest ever winning margin. Fignon, who famously cried on the podium in Paris, had won the Giro in the same year, but his career never quite recovered from the disappointment. Sadly, suffering from cancer he died aged only 50. Nonetheless, he is remembered as a superb rider who, for a brief period, blazed as brightly as any had ever done.

SOUR FACED
French journalists awarded Fignon the Prix Citron, or Lemon Prize, after the 1989 Tour. This was an 'honour' given to the least likeable rider. Naturally an introvert, Fignon later said he found it hard to be accommodating amid all the media attention.

STUDENT TYPE
Fignon's rimless glasses and unruly hair worn in a pigtail gave him the appearance of an academic. Combined with his astute tactical mind, it earnt him the nickname Le Prof, or The Professor, even though he earnt only a D in the French A-level equivalent and aborted his university career.

THE FACTS

Full name **Laurent Patrick Fignon**

Nickname **The Professor**

Date of birth **August 12, 1960**

Died **August 31, 2010**

Birthplace **Paris, France**

Height **5ft 8½in (1.88m)**

THE MAJOR VICTORIES

1990
1989
1988
1987
1986
1985
1984
1983
1982

'You never stop grieving over an event like that; the best you can manage is to contain the effect it has on your mind.'

Fignon on losing the 1989 Tour

2 Critérium International
1 La Flèche Wallonne
2 Milan-San Remo
1 Giro d'Italia
2 Tour de France

THE TEAMS

1982-85
Reynault-Elf

1986-1989
Système U

1990-1991
Castorama

1992-1993
Gatorade

'He had a very, very big talent, much more than anyone recognised. He was one of the few riders who I really admired for his honesty and his frankness.'

Greg LeMond on Fignon.

SPEED FIX

Fignon was unusually candid about drugs. He admitted to using amphetamines when they were widespread in the sport, but insisted he never tried blood-doping when it emerged in the early 1990s and quit when he knew he would not be able to compete with those who did. **'We didn't feel like we were cheating: each of us settled matters with his conscience,'** he said. **'And in any case, everyone did it.'**

Every second counts

The closest ever winning margins at the Giro d'Italia have thrown up some intriguing tales.

Fiorenzo Magni (Ita) beat Ezio Cecchi (Ita) by 11sec, 1948
Story of the race Magni set up his victory with an escape on stage nine into Napoli that opened up a 13-minute gap over chief rivals and compatriots Fausto Coppi, Gino Bartali and Giordano Cottur. The triumph was then secured when Coppi, the reigning champion, quit after winning stage 17 because he was furious with the fans who pushed Magni through the mountains.

Eddy Merckx (Bel) beat Gianbattista Baronchelli (Ita) by 12sec, 1974
Story of the race José Manuel Fuente had looked to be the rider most likely to challenge Merckx – who was chasing his third consecutive victory – but the Spaniard famously forgot to eat on stage 14, then ran out of energy in the mountains and lost the pink jersey to the Belgian. Baronchelli then put up a formidable fight but could never remove Merckx from the overall lead.

Fiorenzo Magni (Ita) beat Fausto Coppi (Ita) by 13sec, 1955
Story of the race Magni trailed Gastone Nencini going into the penultimate stage but cleverly chose a heavier set of tyres for a route that crossed unpaved roads. When Nencini punctured, Magni attacked, took Coppi with him and the pair raced on in a two-up break for 160km to occupy the top two spots on the podium. Poor Nencini finished third on the general classification, four minutes behind.

Ryder Hesjedal (Can) beat Joaquim Rodriguez (Spa) by 16sec, 2012
Story of the race Rodriguez wore the maglia rosa for the six stages leading up to the final one, having performed superbly in the mountains, but his 31-second advantage over Hesjedal was insufficient heading into the final-stage time trial. By overtaking his rival, the Canadian became only the second non-European to win the Giro, and only the second rider ever to take over the leader's jersey on the final day.

Gastone Nencini (Ita) beat Louison Bobet (Fra) by 19sec, 1957
Story of the race Nencini claimed his only overall triumph in the Giro by profiting from the bitter rivalry between Bobet and Charly Gaul. With his previously strong hopes of victory having faded, the Luxembourger assisted Nencini to the point of exhaustion on the final mountain stage – which Gaul ended up winning – to ensure that Bobet could not overtake Nencini on GC. It was the closest the Frenchman went to winning the Giro.

Felice Gimondi (Ita) beat Johan De Muynck (Bel) by 19sec, 1976
Story of the race De Muynck might well have won his first Grand Tour in 1978 had team-mates Roger De Vlaeminck and Ronald De Witte not refused to support him, so furious were the Flandrian pair that De Muynck had usurped De Vlaeminck as team leader. The row allowed Gimondi to close the gap decisively on the final mountain stage when De Muynck crashed while on a descent. He did win the Giro two years later, though.

Giro's iconic climbs

All but one of the Giro d'Italia's major climbs are located in the Dolomites. Only the Stelvio, the iconic Alpine pass, is elsewhere.

Gradient key

0-4%

4-7%

7-10%

+10%

Mortirolo (from Mazzo Valtellina)
Climb length: 11.4km • *Altitude:* 1885m • *Height gain:* 1315m
Average gradient: 11%% • *Maximum gradient:* 18%
Key fact: One of the most feared climbs in bike racing. At the summit is a memorial to Marco Pantani, the Italian who scaled it in the quickest ever time of 42min 40sec in 1994.

Pordoi (from Canazei)
Climb length: 13km • *Altitude:* 2239m • *Height gain:* 786m
Average gradient: 6% • *Maximum gradient:* 7%
Key fact: It has been the Cima Coppi – the title given to the highest mountain on the Giro – on 17 occasions, including in 2016. There is a memorial to Fausto Coppi (Ita) at its summit.

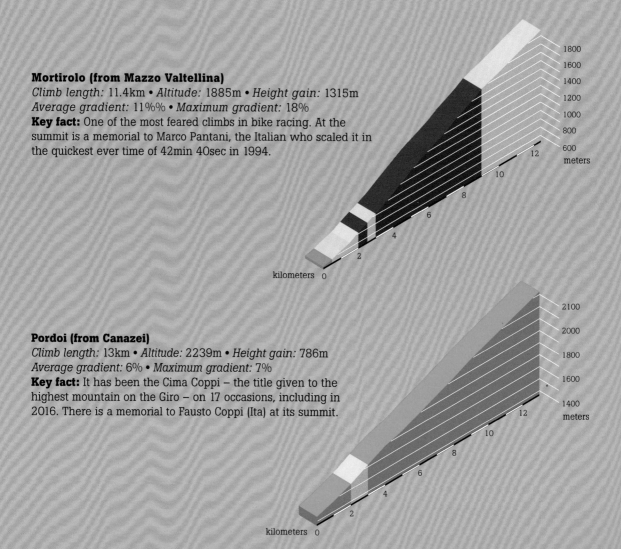

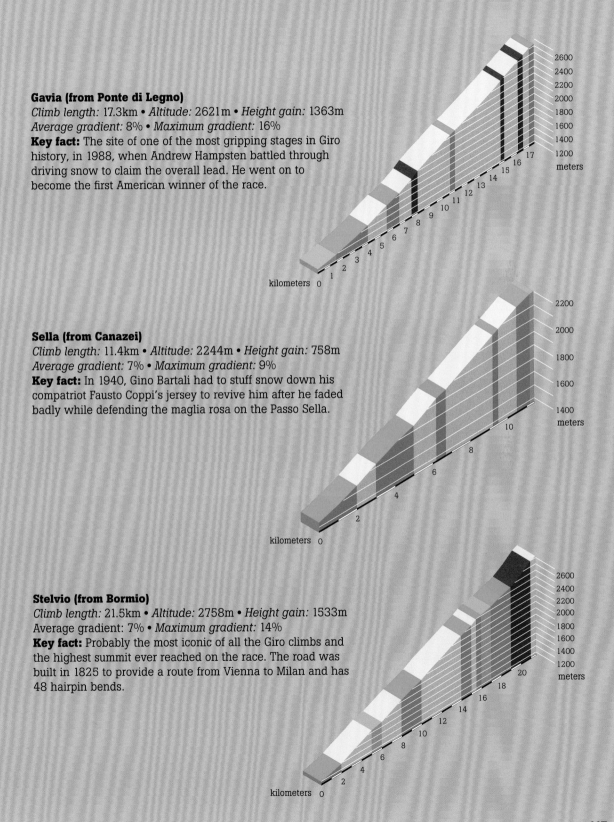

Gavia (from Ponte di Legno)

Climb length: 17.3km • *Altitude:* 2621m • *Height gain:* 1363m
Average gradient: 8% • *Maximum gradient:* 16%

Key fact: The site of one of the most gripping stages in Giro history, in 1988, when Andrew Hampsten battled through driving snow to claim the overall lead. He went on to become the first American winner of the race.

Sella (from Canazei)

Climb length: 11.4km • *Altitude:* 2244m • *Height gain:* 758m
Average gradient: 7% • *Maximum gradient:* 9%

Key fact: In 1940, Gino Bartali had to stuff snow down his compatriot Fausto Coppi's jersey to revive him after he faded badly while defending the maglia rosa on the Passo Sella.

Stelvio (from Bormio)

Climb length: 21.5km • *Altitude:* 2758m • *Height gain:* 1533m
Average gradient: 7% • *Maximum gradient:* 14%

Key fact: Probably the most iconic of all the Giro climbs and the highest summit ever reached on the race. The road was built in 1825 to provide a route from Vienna to Milan and has 48 hairpin bends.

Monument #3
Paris-Roubaix

'The Hell of the North'
First edition: 1896
Distance: 257.5km (2016)

'The Queen of the Classics' is the most coveted of all one-day races in cycling and surely the most difficult, with tough cobbled sectors that create a superb spectacle for the fan and leave even the most adroit competitors cursing a formidably punishing and often dangerous ride. Indeed, many of the top stage-racers now avoid Paris-Roubaix for fear of curtailing their season with injury, but those who win a race that recalls a more primitive time in the sport are assured status among the greats.

Monsieur Paris-Roubaix

Even though Tom Boonen equalled his record of four victories in the race in 2012, Roger De Vlaeminck is still regarded by most as the event's greatest competitor, having competed in it in an era when more of the sport's best riders took part (including Eddy Merckx). He also went close to winning it multiple times: his skill on the cobbles helped him to finish second four times, fifth once, sixth once and seventh twice.

Most victories

4 **Roger De Vlaeminck** (Belgium)
1972, 1974, 1975, 1977
Tom Boonen (Belgium)
2005, 2008, 2009, 2012

3 **Octave Lapize** (France)
1909-1911
Gaston Rebry (Belgium)
1931, 1934, 1935
Rik Van Looy (Belgium)
1961, 1962, 1965
Eddy Merckx (Belgium)
1968, 1970, 1973
Francesco Moser (Italy)
1978-1980
Johan Museeuw (Belgium)
1996, 2000, 2002
Fabian Cancellara (Switzerland)
2006, 2010, 2013

Fastest wins
(average speed)

45.1km/h
Peter Post

44.2km/h
Fabian Cancellara

43.9km/h
Mathew Hayman

27
Number of cobbled sectors in the 2016 edition

THREE OF THE TOUGHEST 'FIVE-STAR' COBBLED SECTORS ☛
(2016)

| 0 | 20 | 40 | 60 | 80 | 100 | 120 |

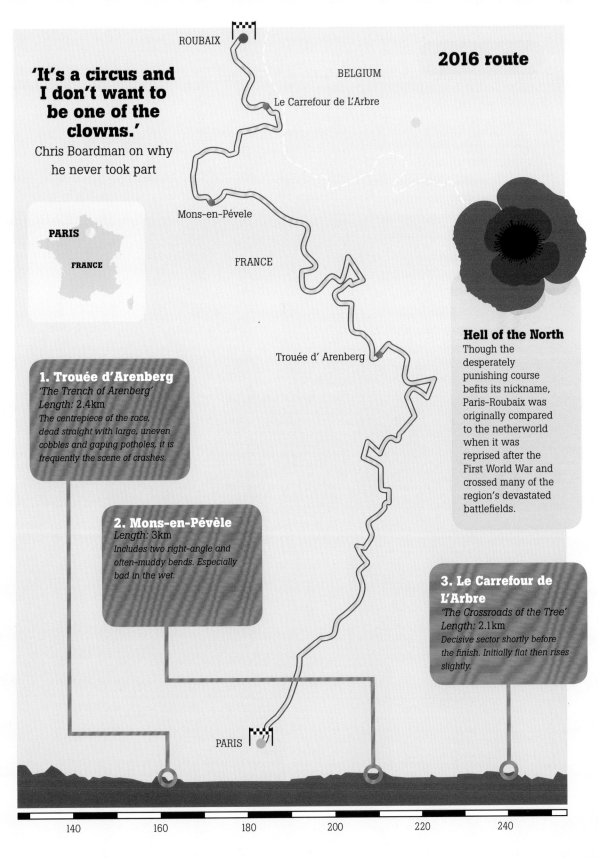

ROUBAIX

2016 route

BELGIUM

Le Carrefour de L'Arbre

'It's a circus and I don't want to be one of the clowns.'

Chris Boardman on why he never took part

PARIS
FRANCE

Mons-en-Pévele

FRANCE

Hell of the North
Though the desperately punishing course befits its nickname, Paris-Roubaix was originally compared to the netherworld when it was reprised after the First World War and crossed many of the region's devastated battlefields.

Trouée d' Arenberg

1. Trouée d'Arenberg
'The Trench of Arenberg'
Length: 2.4km
The centrepiece of the race, dead straight with large, uneven cobbles and gaping potholes, it is frequently the scene of crashes.

2. Mons-en-Pévèle
Length: 3km
Includes two right-angle and often-muddy bends. Especially bad in the wet.

3. Le Carrefour de L'Arbre
'The Crossroads of the Tree'
Length: 2.1km
Decisive sector shortly before the finish. Initially flat then rises slightly.

PARIS

140   160   180   200   220   240

Doping excuses: the best and worst

How well could you spot a doper? Use this quiz to test your knowledge of the most ambitious excuses for failed drug tests.

1

How did the Frenchman Rachel Dard unsuccessfully try to cheat a doping control in an infamous incident after the L'Étoile des Espoirs stage race in 1976?

a) Employed a mechanic to provide a urine sample.

b) Diluted his urine sample with a bottle of Orangina.

c) Tucked a condom of untainted urine in his shorts.

2

The Dutchman Adri van der Poel tested positive for strychnine in 1983. His explanation?

a) He had been handling rat poison after a vermin outbreak at home.

b) He had eaten pigeon pie made with his father's doped racing pigeons.

c) He heard The Rolling Stones dabbled in it and fancied giving it a try.

3

How did Franck Vandenbroucke explain the drugs that police found in a raid on the Belgian rider's house in 2001?

a) They were for his dog.

b) A rival team planted them in his home.

c) He took them off a younger team-mate to prevent him from being tempted by the evils of doping.

4

What did Lithuania's Raimondas Rumsas tell police when they found 37 different medicines – including several banned substances – in his wife Edith's car in 2002?

a) The couple were planning to open a pharmacy.

b) He wanted a few options for his wife's headaches.

c) The drugs were all for his terribly sick mother-in-law.

5

What did the Italian Gilberto Simoni say was the source of the cocaine found in his system in 2002?

a) Contaminated sweeties given to him by his aunt.

b) Licking his fingers while counting lira notes.

c) He kissed the wrong woman at a nightclub.

6

How did the American Tyler Hamilton account for the two types of blood in his system after the 2004 Vuelta a España?

a) He had eaten a large portion of steak tartare shortly before his test.

b) He had absorbed DNA from his unborn twin.

c) He realised the error of his ways and admitted he was part of a systematic blood-doping regime.

7

How did Floyd Landis account for his abnormally high testosterone levels after stage 17 of the 2006 Tour de France?

a) He got drunk on whisky after an exhausting day in the mountains.

b) He celebrated his stage victory with a night of vigorous love-making.

c) He claimed American heroes were just built that way.

8

What did Italy's Mauro Santambrogio say was the reason for his positive test for testosterone in October 2014, which happened while he was banned for EPO?

a) He thought you could do what you want if you were banned.

b) The substance was taken to help with his erectile dysfunction.

c) His long-term plan was to get away with doping by becoming a whistle-blower.

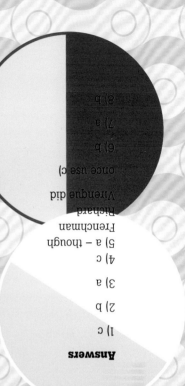

Answers

1) c

2) b

3) a

4) c

5) a – though Frenchman Richard Virenque did once use c)

6) b

7) a

8) b

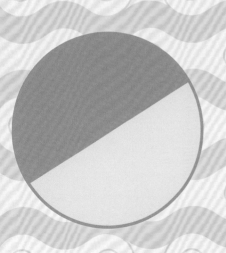

121

Not over the hill

Cycling is mostly a young man's sport but a few have defied the march of time in style.

Most Grand Tour finishes
Eduardo Chozas (Spa), 1980-1993
6 Tours, 7 Giros, 13 Vueltas

007
Guy Nulens (Belgium)
15 starts, 1980-94, 13 finishes
DNF: 1980, 1983
Senior moment: A perennial domestique, Nulens enjoyed only one significant victory in a 16-year career, at the Star of Bessèges stage-race in France.

006
Viatcheslav Ekimov (Russia)
15 starts, 15 finishes, 1990-98, 2000-04, 2006
Senior moment: The peloton paid tribute to Ekimov on the final stage of his last Tour by allowing him to cross the finish line first on the opening lap of the Champs-Élysées.

005
Lucien Van Impe (Belgium)
15 starts, 15 finishes, 1969-81, 1983, 1985
Senior moment: At a crucial stage of the 1977 Tour, Van Impe forgot to eat before scaling Alpe d'Huez, squandering his chance of overall victory.

003
Jens Voigt (Germany)
17 starts, 1998-2013, 13 finishes
DNF: 2003, 2005, 2009
Senior moment: Voigt is known for the catchphrase with which he addresses his own body parts: 'Shut up, legs!'

Most participations in the Tour de France

008
Christophe Moreau (France)
15 starts, 1996-2010, 11 finishes
DNF: 2001-02, 2008
DQ: 1998
Senior moment: Moreau married the podium girl who presented him with the yellow jersey after he won the prologue at the 2001 Tour.

15 STARTS

002
George Hincapie (USA)
17 starts, 1996-2012, 13 finishes
DNF: 1997 Disqualified: 2004-06
Senior moment: After 19 years of denying doping as a professional, Hincapie also thought it wise to come clean only after he had retired in 2012.

17 STARTS

STARTS

001
Stuart O'Grady (Australia)
17 starts, 1997-2013,
15 finishes
Did not finish: 2000, 2007
Senior moment: O'Grady was a vocal critic of doping in the 1990s and early 2000s. In 2013, he remembered he had actually taken drugs and confessed.

33

Most Grand Tour participations
Matteo Tosatto (Ita)
(33 at the last count),
1997-2016
12 Tours, 12 Giros,
9 Vueltas

004
Joop Zoetemelk
(Netherlands)
16 starts, 16 finishes,
1970-73, 1975-86
Senior moment: Zoetemelk is the oldest ever World Road Race champion, having won the title aged 38 in 1985.

Chris Horner became the oldest ever winner of a Grand Tour when the American triumphed at the 2013 Vuelta a España aged 41. He battled back from a superbug that attacked his lungs in 2015 to sign up for the Lupus Racing Team in 2016.

36
The Belgian **Firmin Lambot** is the oldest ever winner of the Tour de France, having triumphed aged 36 in 1922.

* Figures correct up and including the 2015 Tour.

The toughest Tour

The 1926 Tour de France is often described as the toughest in the history of the race – with good reason. It was the longest ever, yet had fewer stages than previous years, the weather was frequently dreadful and riders battled across unpaved roads on a route that essentially formed a 'lap' of the country. Two-thirds of them were racing alone, too, without the support of a team.

Winner: Lucien Buysse

Born: Sept 11, 1892
Birthplace: East Flanders, Belgium
Team: Automoto

Role: Started the race as a domestique to reigning champion Ottavio Bottecchia, but the Italian withdrew during the tenth stage.
Family tragedy: Some historians believe that Buysse almost withdrew after the third stage on being told that his daughter had died, while others believe she passed away a fortnight before the Tour.
Story of his race: Buysse never relinquished the yellow jersey after claiming it with his courageous triumph on stage 10, which he followed up with victory the following day in the mountains.

EPIC STAGE

Stage 10 has been described as the most gruelling in the Tour's history.

Distance: 326km
Major cols: Aubisque, Tourmalet, Aspin, Peyresourde
Starting riders: 76
Withdrawals: 22
Winner: Lucien Buysse
Winning time: 17hr 12min 4sec

Story of the stage: Constant rain fell while the riders crossed the mountains, which meant that only nine of them finished within an hour of Buysse and only 46 made it to the finish line by 10.20pm, which should have been the cut-off point. The Tour organisers extended that deadline to midnight, by which time 54 riders had finished.

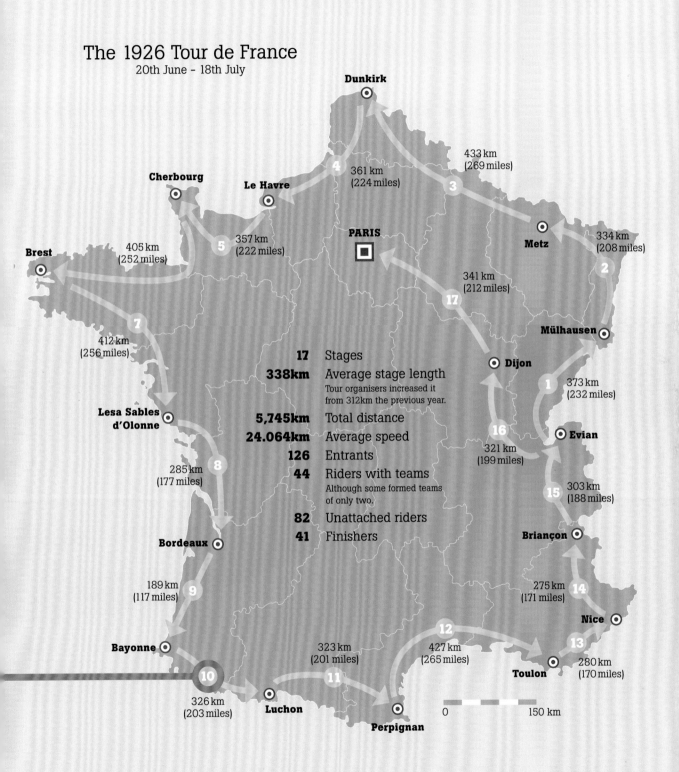

The 1926 Tour de France
20th June – 18th July

Dunkirk

433 km
(269 miles)

Cherbourg

Le Havre

361 km
(224 miles)

PARIS

Metz

334 km
(208 miles)

Brest

405 km
(252 miles)

357 km
(222 miles)

5

4

3

2

341 km
(212 miles)

17

Mülhausen

7

412 km
(256 miles)

Dijon

Lesa Sables
d'Olonne

17 Stages
338km Average stage length
Tour organisers increased it
from 312km the previous year.

5,745km Total distance
24.064km Average speed
126 Entrants
44 Riders with teams
Although some formed teams
of only two.

82 Unattached riders
41 Finishers

1

373 km
(232 miles)

16

Evian

8

285 km
(177 miles)

321 km
(199 miles)

303 km
(188 miles)

15

Bordeaux

Briançon

9

189 km
(117 miles)

275 km
(171 miles)

14

Nice

Bayonne

10

12

427 km
(265 miles)

13

Toulon

280 km
(170 miles)

323 km
(201 miles)

11

326 km
(203 miles)

Luchon

Perpignan

0   150 km

ICON Jeannie Longo

The grande dame of French cycling boasts a palmares that surpasses every other woman except Beryl Burton. Longo won 59 French national titles and has 13 world titles. As adept in stage races as she was in one-day events and on the track, Longo enjoyed phenomenal longevity too, having competed across three decades and in seven Olympic Games. She retired under a cloud in 2011 but remains among the most revered riders in the sport.

58

Number of national titles that Longo won between 1979 and 2011.

49

Longo was aged 49 when she finished fourth in the time trial and 24th in the road race at her final Olympics in 2008. The winner of the latter race, Britain's Nicole Cooke, was aged only one when Longo competed in her first Games.

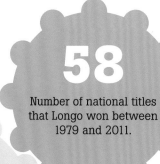

THE FACTS

Full name **Jeannie Longo**

Nickname **The Cannibal**

Date of birth **October 31, 1958**

Birthplace **Annecy, France**

Height **5ft 5in (1.65m)**

THE MAJOR VICTORIES

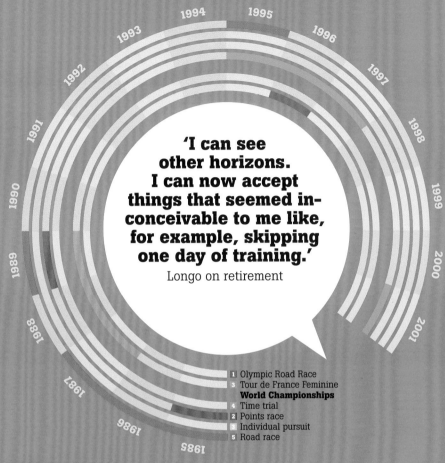

1994
1995
1993
1996
1992
1997
1991
1998
1990
1999
1989
2000
1988
2001
1987
1986
1985

'I can see other horizons. I can now accept things that seemed inconceivable to me like, for example, skipping one day of training.'

Longo on retirement

1 Olympic Road Race
3 Tour de France Feminine
World Championships
4 Time trial
2 Points race
3 Individual pursuit
5 Road race

OTHER ACHIEVEMENTS AT WORLD CHAMPIONSHIPS

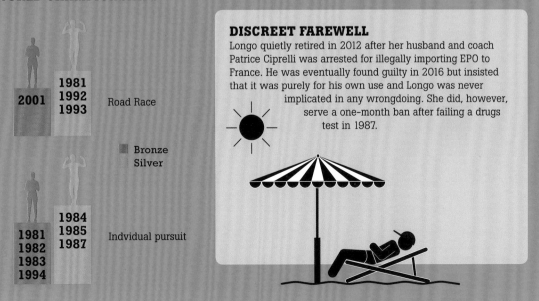

2001

1981
1992
1993

Road Race

Bronze
Silver

1981
1982
1983
1994

1984
1985
1987

Indvidual pursuit

DISCREET FAREWELL

Longo quietly retired in 2012 after her husband and coach Patrice Ciprelli was arrested for illegally importing EPO to France. He was eventually found guilty in 2016 but insisted that it was purely for his own use and Longo was never implicated in any wrongdoing. She did, however, serve a one-month ban after failing a drugs test in 1987.

Lance Armstrong in his own words

Lance Armstrong spent years forcibly denying all accusations that he doped during his career only to make a sharp about-turn in 2013, after the US Anti-Doping Agency gathered a huge amount of evidence incriminating him. He was subsequently stripped of his seven Tour de France titles.

2012
" I have never doped. I have competed as an endurance athlete for 25 years with no spike in performance, passed more than 500 drug tests and never failed one "

1999
" I have been on my deathbed, and I'm not stupid. I can emphatically say I am not on drugs "

2000
" We are completely innocent. We run a very clean and professional team that has been singled out due to our success ... Before this ordeal I had never heard of Actovegin [the performance-enhancing drug] "

2001
" The simple truth is that we outwork everyone. But when you perform at a higher level in a race, you get questions about doping "

2013

I didn't invent the [drug] culture, but I didn't try to stop the culture, and that's my mistake, and that's what I have to be sorry [for] and that's what the sport is now paying the price for because of that...

2013

I looked up the definition of cheat. The definition of cheat is to gain an advantage over a rival or foe. I didn't do that. I viewed it as a level playing field

2015

If I was racing in 2015, no, I wouldn't do it again because I don't think you have to. But if you take me back to 1995, when doping was completely pervasive, I would probably do it again

2015

I think there has to be a winner, I'm just saying that as a fan. I feel like I won those Tours

2004

I have never had a single positive doping test, and I do not take performance-enhancing drugs

2005

Why would I enter into a sport and then dope myself up and risk my life again? That's crazy. I would never do that. No way

2010

As long as I live, I will deny it. There was absolutely no way I forced people, encouraged people, told people, helped people, facilitated. Absolutely not. One hundred per cent

2011

Twenty-plus-year career, 500 drug controls worldwide, in and out of competition. Never a failed test. I rest my case

129

Speed peaks

The overall average speed at the Tour de France rose steadily through the 20th century but dropped after the blood-boosting era reached its zenith in the mid-2000s and has plateaued in recent years – perhaps the race has found the limit of cyclist capability?

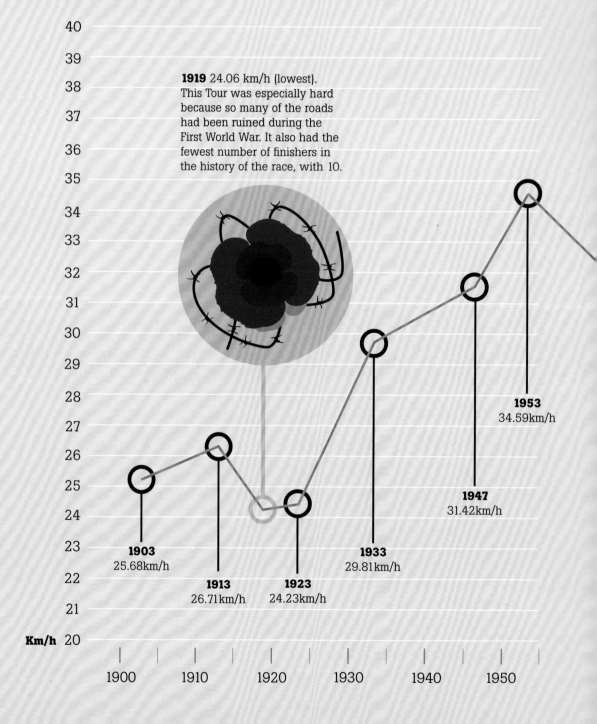

1919 24.06 km/h (lowest). This Tour was especially hard because so many of the roads had been ruined during the First World War. It also had the fewest number of finishers in the history of the race, with 10.

1903 25.68km/h

1913 26.71km/h

1923 24.23km/h

1933 29.81km/h

1947 31.42km/h

1953 34.59km/h

Km/h 20

1900   1910   1920   1930   1940   1950

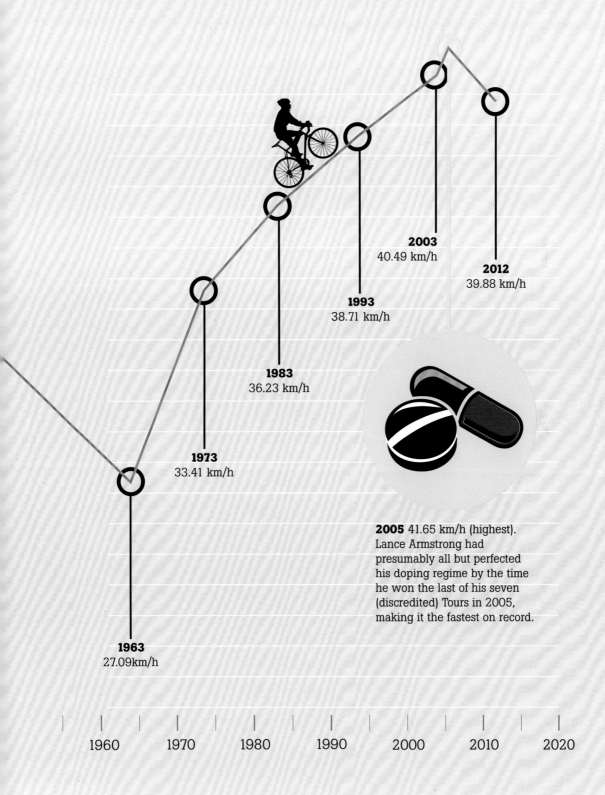

2003
40.49 km/h

2012
39.88 km/h

1993
38.71 km/h

1983
36.23 km/h

1973
33.41 km/h

2005 41.65 km/h (highest). Lance Armstrong had presumably all but perfected his doping regime by the time he won the last of his seven (discredited) Tours in 2005, making it the fastest on record.

1963
27.09km/h

1960   1970   1980   1990   2000   2010   2020

Quit while you're ahead

Up until 2016, sixteen riders had withdrawn from the Tour de France while leading the general classification.

Francis Pélissier (Fra)
Stage 6, 1927
The leader of the Dilecta-Wolber team – brother of Tour winner Henri and Tour stage winner Charles – had worn the yellow jersey for the first five stages before he pulled out through sickness.

Victor Fontan (Fra)
Stage 10, 1929
At a time when riders had to start and finish a stage on the one bike, Fontan was disqualified after his forks broke in a crash on the Pyrenees. His plight prompted the rule to be dropped a year later.

Sylvère Maes (Bel)
Stage 16, 1937
The then-reigning champion was part of the Belgian team that withdrew because of abuse they had suffered from French fans, which included stone-throwing and pepper being hurled in their eyes.

Fiorenzo Magni (Ita)
Stage 11, 1950
The two Italian national teams withdrew because they had been harangued and assaulted by French fans who were furious with Magni's compatriot Gino Bartali for allegedly causing home hero Jean Robic to crash.

Bernard Hinault (Fra)
Stage 12, 1980
'The Badger' suffered intermittent knee problems throughout his career and was denied a third consecutive Tour victory when he was hit by the complaint after the first set of mountain stages.

Pascal Simon (Fra)
Stage 17, 1983
Simon crashed and broke his shoulder blade on stage 11 while leading the general classification. He managed to hold on to the yellow jersey for six days, until eventually the pain became too much.

Rolf Sorensen (Den)
Stage 5, 1991
One of the most successful ever Danish riders fractured his clavicle when he crashed in the final kilometre of the fifth stage. He made it to the stage finish but was unable to restart the following morning.

Stéphane Heulot (Fra)
Stage 7, 1996
Heulot was forced to abandon in tears while on the Cormet de Roseland climb. He was suffering from knee trouble amid fog and torrential rain that forced several riders to crash in the Alps.

Wim Van Est (Ned)
Stage 13, 1951
The Dutchman ran out of road and crashed into a 150ft, near sheer-faced ravine on the descent of the Aubisque. Amazingly, he suffered only slight injuries but lost so much time that he had to abandon.

Bernard van de Kerkhove (Bel)
Stage 9, 1965
The Belgian, whose surname had 27 different spellings and had been in yellow for two stages before his withdrawal – he was one of several riders to suffer an upset stomach on the first mountain stage.

Luis Ocaña (Spa)
Stage 14, 1971
The Spaniard was leading Eddy Merckx by more than eight minutes in the overall standings when he was forced to quit the race following one of the most infamous falls in Tour history while descending the Col de Menté.

Michel Pollentier (Bel)
Stage 16, 1978
Expelled for attempting to cheat a doping test with a fake urine sample. Pollentier's less-than-sophisticated trick was to eject untainted urine through a tube connected to a condom hidden aunder his arm.

Chris Boardman (GB)
Stage 2, 1998
The Briton suffered a debilitating head injury when he crashed 24 hours after winning the prologue. Boardman was the only rider to wear yellow on the 1998 Tour who was not later implicated in doping.

Michael Rasmussen (Den)
Stage 16, 2007
Fired by his team after they accused him of lying about his reasons for missing drug tests earlier in the season. He served a two-year ban as a result and later admitted to taking banned substances.

Fabian Cancellara (Swi)
Stage 3, 2015
'Spartacus' suffered two fractured vertebrae in his spine after he was involved in one of the worst crashes in Tour history. Five other riders were forced to withdraw as a result of it.

Tony Martin (Ger)
Stage 7, 2015
Suffered a broken collarbone in a crash within the final kilometre of stage six. During a week littered with pile-ups, Martin made it to the finish line but was unable to start the next morning.

Kings of the mountains

Any list that compares athletes from across the generations is an imperfect one and doubtless many fans will disagree with this list of the 10 finest climbers in history, named in chronological order. But surely no one could confidently bet against anyone from this list succeeding over the toughest mountain passes.

GINO BARTALI

Italy
Professional career:
1935-1954

- 1938, 1948
- 1935, 1936, 1937, 1939, 1940, 1946, 1947

FAUSTO COPPI

Italy
Professional career:
1938-1959

- 1949, 1952
- 1948, 1949, 1954

LOUISON BOBET

France
Professional career:
1947-1962

- 1950
- 1951

CHARLY GAUL

Luxembourg
Professional career:
1953-1965

- 1955, 1956
- 1956, 1959

FEDERICO BAHAMONTES

Spain
Professional career:
1953-1965

- 1954, 1958, 1959, 1962, 1963, 1964
- 1959

Memorable climb
Ahead of the 13th stage of the 1948 Tour, the Italian prime minister pleaded with Bartali to try to win the next day's stage to distract the Italian public from the threat of civil war. Bartali responded by winning three mountain stages in a row and eventually the race itself.

Memorable climb
On the 17th stage of the 1949 Giro, Coppi attacked on the first of five category-one climbs and held his lead for the 192km that remained of the stage.

Memorable climb
On stage 18 of the 1953 Tour, the first of the three Tours that Bobet won in succession, the Breton launched a brilliant solo breakaway on the Col d'Izoard. He then held off the peloton to win the stage by more than five minutes. The victory gave Bobet the yellow jersey and he kept hold of it until Paris.

Memorable climb
At the 1956 Giro, Gaul cut a 16-minute deficit to overall leader Pasquale Fornara with his 14km ascent of Monte Bondone amid freezing weather, helping him to win the race. 'The Angel of the Mountains' was so cold that he had to be cut from his jersey afterwards.

Memorable climb
The mountain time-trial at the 1959 Tour when Bahamontes, having finally been persuaded to target the general classification, secured the stage victory that was key to the Eagle of Toledo's' one overall Tour triumph.

'Kings of the Mountains' titles
- ■ Tour de France
- ■ Giro d'Italia
- ■ Vuelta a España

JULIO JIMÉNEZ
Spain
Professional career:
1959–1969

- ■ 1965, 1966, 1967
- ■ 1963, 1964, 1965

EDDY MERCKX
Belgium
Professional career:
1965–1978

- ■ 1969, 1970
- ■ 1968

LUCIEN VAN IMPE
Belgium
Professional career:
1969–1987

- ■ 1971, 1972, 1975, 1977, 1981, 1983
- ■ 1982, 1983

LUIS HERRERA
Colombia
Professional career:
1985–1992

- ■ 1985, 1987
- ■ 1989
- ■ 1987, 1991

MARCO PANTANI
Italy
Professional career:
1991–2003

- ■ 1998

Memorable climb
Stage 16 of the 1966 Tour when, with a chasing group including Jacques Anquetil and Raymond Poulidor in pursuit, Jiménez held on to a solo breakaway over the Télégraphe and Galibier climbs to win the stage by more than two minutes.

Memorable climb
On stage 17 of the 1969 Tour, which featured four epic climbs: the Peyresourde, the Aspin, the Tourmalet and the Aubisque. Merckx attacked on the Tourmalet, split the peloton and eventually won the stage after a 140km solo breakaway.

Memorable climb
A career-defining attack on stage 14 of the 1976 Tour when his team manager Cyrille Guimard is said to have threatened to run Van Impe off the road if he did not give chase to Luis Ocaña over the Peyresourde. The Belgian not only hunted the Spaniard down but won the stage and the Tour.

Memorable climb
On the Alpe d'Huez stage of the 1984 Tour, when the debutant Herrera surged away from the field to become the first amateur to win a Tour stage.

Memorable climb
Pantani could blow pelotons apart with his climbing ability, an asset that helped him to win eight Tour stages. Few of those victories were better than the one on the Queen stage of the 1994 Giro when he attacked on the Mortirolo climb and held his lead to win by a full two minutes.

Marginal gains

The Tour de France has produced some memorably tight finishes on the general classification. These nine were the closest of all in the modern era.

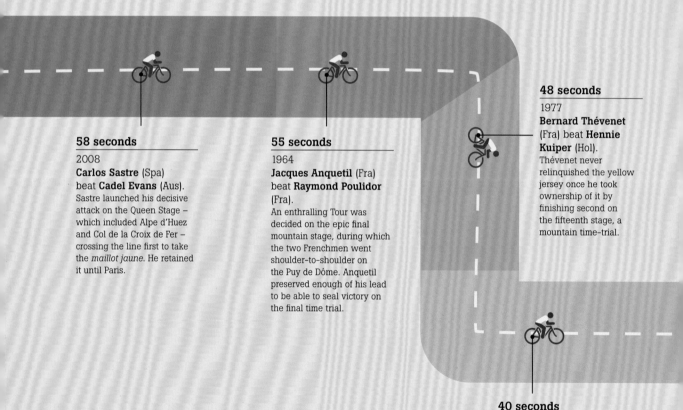

58 seconds
2008
Carlos Sastre (Spa) beat **Cadel Evans** (Aus). Sastre launched his decisive attack on the Queen Stage – which included Alpe d'Huez and Col de la Croix de Fer – crossing the line first to take the *maillot jaune*. He retained it until Paris.

55 seconds
1964
Jacques Anquetil (Fra) beat **Raymond Poulidor** (Fra).
An enthralling Tour was decided on the epic final mountain stage, during which the two Frenchmen went shoulder-to-shoulder on the Puy de Dôme. Anquetil preserved enough of his lead to be able to seal victory on the final time trial.

48 seconds
1977
Bernard Thévenet (Fra) beat **Hennie Kuiper** (Hol). Thévenet never relinquished the yellow jersey once he took ownership of it by finishing second on the fifteenth stage, a mountain time-trial.

40 seconds
1987
Stephen Roche (Ire) beat **Pedro Delgado** (Spa). Roche stayed in touch with Delgado with several masterful rides in the mountains, then used his superior time-trial ability to trump the Spaniard in the final time-trial.

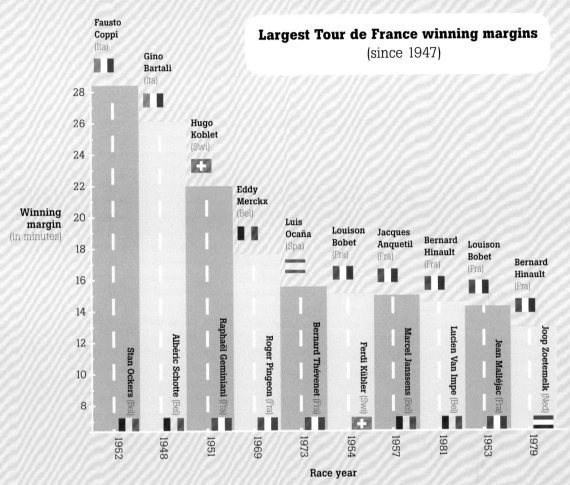

Largest Tour de France winning margins
(since 1947)

Winning margin
(in minutes)

Fausto Coppi (Ita) — Stan Ockers (Bel) — 1952
Gino Bartali (Ita) — Albéric Schotte (Bel) — 1948
Hugo Koblet (Swi) — Raphaël Geminiani (Fra) — 1951
Eddy Merckx (Bel) — Roger Pingeon (Fra) — 1969
Luis Ocaña (Spa) — Bernard Thévenet (Fra) — 1973
Louison Bobet (Fra) — Ferdi Kübler (Swi) — 1954
Jacques Anquetil (Fra) — Marcel Janssens (Bel) — 1957
Bernard Hinault (Fra) — Lucien Van Impe (Bel) — 1981
Louison Bobet (Fra) — Jean Malléjac (Fra) — 1953
Bernard Hinault (Fra) — Joop Zoetemelk (Ned) — 1979

Race year

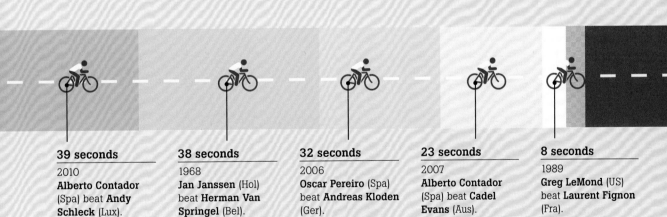

39 seconds

2010
Alberto Contador (Spa) beat **Andy Schleck** (Lux). Contador was later stripped of the title.

38 seconds

1968
Jan Janssen (Hol) beat **Herman Van Springel** (Bel). Yet again the final time-trial was decisive, with Janssen overtaking his Belgian rival on it on the last day.

32 seconds

2006
Oscar Pereiro (Spa) beat **Andreas Kloden** (Ger). Pereiro was actually overtaken by Floyd Landis on the penultimate stage but the American was stripped of the title retrospectively for doping.

23 seconds

2007
Alberto Contador (Spa) beat **Cadel Evans** (Aus). Contador dug in to hold off Evans and third-placed Levi Leipheimer (USA) on the penultimate day's time-trial. The 31 seconds that separated the trio was the shortest time-gap in history for the podium finishers.

8 seconds

1989
Greg LeMond (US) beat **Laurent Fignon** (Fra). LeMond overtook Fignon in the general classification only on the final-day time trial, leaving the home favourite tearful on the podium.

ICON **Greg LeMond**

Grand Tour legend, all-American hero, technical trailblazer and anti-doping scourge of the establishment, Greg LeMond has filled many roles since he emerged on the professional scene in the early 1980s. Raised on the slopes of the Sierra Nevada, he is the only one of his countrymen ever to win the Tour de France (and not be stripped of it) and one of only four men to double up with the World Road-Race title in the same year. He was also always at the cutting edge of new technologies and one of the first major riders to speak out in opposition to the blood doping that overtook the sport towards the end of his career. Now owner of a global bike business, he still holds the sport to account, whether in his criticisms of its administration or of those riders who do not abide by his strict ethical code.

'I love the sport. Faith in the sport being totally clean? I've got to be realistic and say I don't know if that's possible. The question is, do people really care? I think they do.'

LeMond, 2012

$1,000,000

LeMond was the first cyclist to sign a million-dollar contract when he joined the French team La Vie Claire in 1984 in a deal that is credited with transforming the salary structure of the sport

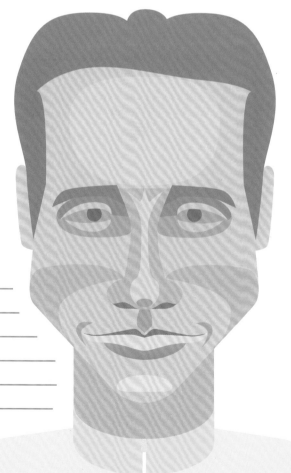

THE FACTS

Full name **Gregory James LeMond**

Nickname **L'Americain/Le Monster**

Date of birth **June 26, 1961**

Birthplace **Lakewood, California**

Height **5ft 10in (1.78m)**

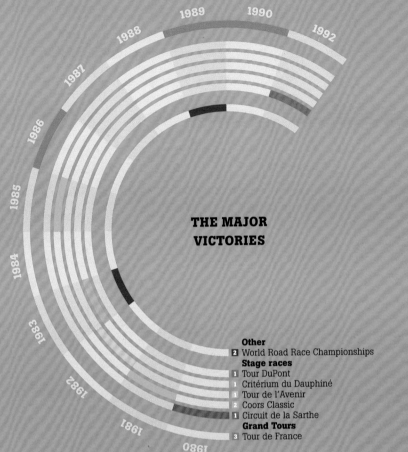

THE MAJOR VICTORIES

1980
1981
1982
1983
1984
1985
1986
1987
1988
1989
1990
1992

Other
[2] World Road Race Championships
Stage races
[1] Tour DuPont
[1] Critérium du Dauphiné
[1] Tour de l'Avenir
[2] Coors Classic
[1] Circuit de la Sarthe
Grand Tours
[3] Tour de France

THE TEAMS

1981-84
Renault-Elf-Gitane

1985-1987
La Vie Claire

1988
PDM-Ultima-Concorde

1989
ADR

1990-94
Z-Tomasso

BREAKING THE MOULD
LeMond was a pioneer of carbon-fibre frames and he scored the first Tour de France victory on one when he beat his team-mate Bernard Hinault to triumph in 1986.

BACK FROM THE BRINK
LeMond's most memorable victory came in the 1989 Tour de France when he beat Laurent Fignon on the final stage, a time trial, to wipe out the Frenchman's lead on the general classification and triumph by eight seconds – the narrowest margin in the history of the race. The achievement was especially remarkable because LeMond was contesting his first Tour since suffering life-threatening injuries when he was accidently shot with an airgun.

Riding their luck

Perhaps it is because there is so much that cyclists cannot control in a race that they make for a superstitious bunch and so often try to make their own luck.

Viatcheslav Ekimov (Rus)
It is common practice for the rider given number 13 in a race to be allowed to turn it upside down and back to front. Others such as Ekimov, Armstrong's super-domestique, simply refused to wear the number altogether.

Silly seasoning...
The fear that spilled salt summons the devil is perhaps the most widespread superstition on the Grand Tours. Italian riders are so scared of Beelzebub that they refuse to pass shakers by hand and will only pick them up from the table, while others use only personal shakers at team meals.

Sir Bradley Wiggins (GB)
The 2012 Tour de France champion refused to shave off his 'lucky' sideburns before his Olympic bid that summer and went on to win time-trial gold. When eventually he did lose them in November of that year, he was hit by a van while riding and suffered rib injuries.

... Or maybe not
In 2002, Danish rider Michael Sandstod attempted to disprove the salt superstition at the Tour de France when he deliberately knocked over a salt shaker at dinner. He crashed the next day, breaking eight ribs, fracturing his shoulder and puncturing his lung.

Tyler Hamilton (USA)
At the 2003 Tour of Holland Hamilton, a former team-mate of Lance Armstrong, forgot the bottle of holy water he carried in every race and suffered a terrible crash.

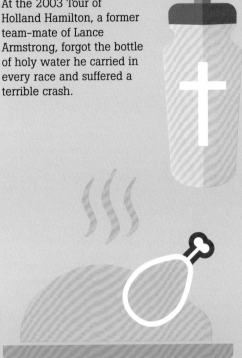

Bart Wellens (Bel)
This cyclo-cross rider insisted on eating a pigeon the night before every important race, though whether that helped him to the world title in 2003 and 2004 is hard to say.

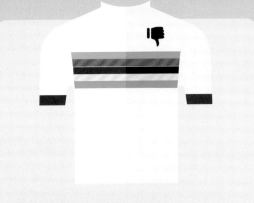

Curse of the rainbow jersey
Every cyclist covets the world champion's jersey but several winners of it have suffered ill fortune, from the Belgian pair Stan Ockers, who died following a crash a year after his triumph in 1955, and Jempi Monseré, the 1970 champion who suffered the same fate, to Paolo Bettini, whose brother died travelling to celebrate the Italian rider's 2006 victory.

The figures add up...
Statistics support belief that the rainbow jersey is jinxed. In 2015, the British Medical Journal published a study that revealed that world champions would win, on average, 5.04 times in the year ahead of their victory, 3.96 times while wearing the rainbow jersey and 3.47 the year after.

Lance Armstrong (USA)
The disgraced American insisted that he finished every stage of the Tour de France on the bike that he started it, forcing mechanics to carry out some swift repairs. He also refused to wear the leader's traditional yellow helmet until the final stage.

Mark Cavendish (GB)
Perhaps it is not only the Manxman's occasional emotional volatility that makes reporters wary of approaching him on the morning of a race. He refuses to shower then, too.

Stranger than fiction

Cycling has produced some fascinating literature.
Here is a selection of the best life stories.

BIKIE
by Charlie Woods, 2001

Often overlooked in lists of the best cycling memoirs, this is a charming account of one amateur's love affair with the sport. With a lyrical turn of phrase, Woods traces his relationship with the sport that began as a child of 1950s London and continued into late middle-age. By working in his reflections on cycling's changing cultural role, it serves as social history and a touchingly evocative memoir.

A ROUGH RIDE
by Paul Kimmage, 1990

A former professional rider, Kimmage suffered stinging rebuke from many fellow riders when he wrote this account of life as a domestique. They believed that the Irishman had committed the unforgivable sin of 'spitting in the soup' by revealing that drug-taking was endemic in the sport. The public, however, realised its value and this superb book set Kimmage up for a successful, second career as a sports writer.

BREAKING THE CHAIN
by Willy Voet, 1999

Voet was the Festina team soigneur whom police stopped while he was driving to the 1998 Tour de France with a boot-load of performance-enhancing drugs. The discovery led to an infamously damning police investigation and, ultimately, to a memoir that reveals in detail just what went on behind the scenes, from every drug administered to accounts of how they were obtained, mixed and concealed.

PUT ME BACK ON MY BIKE: IN SEARCH OF TOM SIMPSON
by William Fotheringham, 2002

The definitive story of a great British cyclist. Fotheringham travels to Avignon to study the medical reports on Simpon's tragic death on Mont Ventoux, sits down with Simpson's widow as she reads his peers' messages of condolences for the first time and, in speaking to the members of the cycling community who knew him best, ensures that Simpson's life will be remembered for much more than his death.

FLYING SCOTSMAN

by Graeme Obree, 2003

By the time that Obree came to publish this book, his wonderfully innovative (and successful) assaults on the Hour Record using a home-made bike were well known, but the battle with clinical depression that eventually drove him to attempt suicide was not. This searingly honest account of his struggles and professional achievements was one of the first to highlight the potential emotional cost of elite sport.

IN SEARCH OF ROBERT MILLAR

by Richard Moore, 2007

Written when Millar was still Britain's most successful rider on the Tour de France, Moore attempts both to tell the story of the Scotsman's singular career and shed light on a fiercely private, even inscrutable individual. Given that Millar went to ground shortly after his retirement, this is no mean task but, through detailed research, Moore manages it with aplomb and finishes with an intriguing email exchange with the man himself.

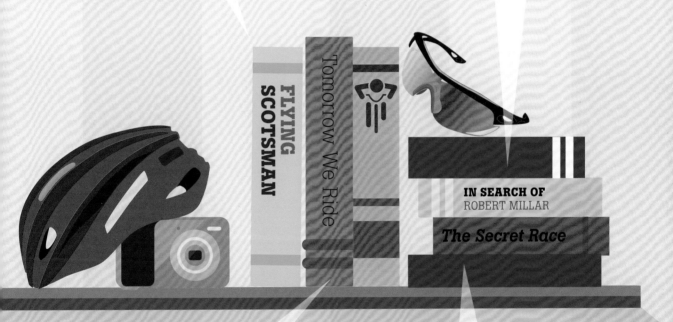

TOMORROW WE RIDE

by Jean Bobet, 2004

Published when Bobet was 74, this unusual but charming book beautifully evokes the world of professional bike racing in the 1950s through the story of two brothers. The elder, Louison, was a legend of the sport, a triple Tour de France champion, while the author was no mean rider himself, winning Paris-Nice in 1955, but spent most of his days riding in his brother's service before embarking on a writing career.

THE SECRET RACE

by Tyler Hamilton, 2012

Published with impeccable timing to coincide with the US Anti-Doping Agency's damning report into Lance Armstrong's doping regime, this ghosted autobiography by his former team-mate serves both as a compelling account of what life was like under the disgraced American's aegis and as an intriguing assessment of a deeply flawed character. It was deservedly named *William Hill Sports Book of the Year*.

Size guide

The ideal stage-race rider is said to be lean and of medium height, but this selection of elite cyclists proves there is no ideal body-shape if you want to be successful.

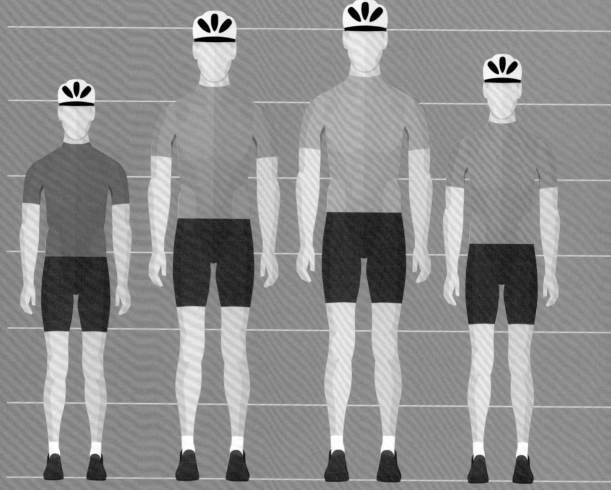

JEAN ROBIC
Height: 5ft 3in
Weight: 9st 6lb
Bodily fact: The 1947 Tour de France champion is the shortest ever winner of the race, though his waif-like frame did not always work in his favour. In 1953, he took on a lead-filled bidon to help him descend more quickly.

MIGUEL INDURAIN
Height: 6ft 2in
Weight: 12st 3lb
Bodily fact: The five-time Tour winner shed a stone when he was 23, on the advice of a sports doctor. His career picked up soon afterwards. He finished the Tour for the first time in the same year and went on to become a superstar of the sport.

MAGNUS BACKSTEDT
Height: 6ft 4in
Weight: 14st 8lb
Bodily fact: The Swede is said to be the heaviest rider ever to complete the Tour, having finished two of the seven editions that he entered. He was more suited to the Classics, winning the 2004 Paris-Roubaix.

LEONARDO PIEPOLI
Height: 5ft 7in
Weight: 8st 7lb
Bodily fact: Piepoli is often cited as the lightest rider to finish the Tour, certainly in the modern era. His especially slender frame helped him to win the climber's classification at the 2007 Giro d'Italia.

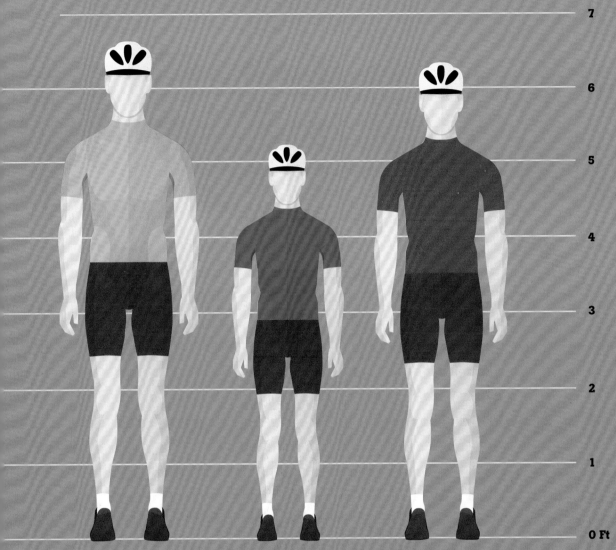

7

6

5

4

3

2

1

0 Ft

JOHAN VAN SUMMEREN
Height: 6ft 6in
Weight: 11st 14lb
Bodily fact: Van
Summeren is the tallest
ever rider to complete the
Tour, managing it eight
of the nine times he took
part. The highlight of his
career was to win the
2011 Paris-Roubaix.

SAMUEL DUMOULIN
Height: 5ft 2.5in
Weight: 8st 12lb
Bodily fact: Dumoulin
is thought to be the
shortest man to have
ridden the Tour, though
he still packed a punch.
The Frenchman won
stage three in 2008 after
a breakaway that lasted
almost 200km.

BRADLEY WIGGINS
Height: 6ft 3in
Weight: 11st 3lb
Bodily fact: The 2012 Tour
de France champion is said
to be the tallest ever winner
of the race. He was also
known for his ability to gain
and lose a lot of weight to
meet his goals. For the 2016
Olympics, he put on two
stone to gain the muscle
power needed to compete
in the team pursuit.

Monument #4
Liège-Bastogne-Liège

'La Doyenne' – The Old Lady
First edition: 1892
Distance: 242km (2016)

Affectionately known as The Old Lady because it is the oldest Classic, Liège-Bastogne-Liège might not be the most prestigious Monument but it is the most popular with riders because it provides the best all-round examination of their abilities, with both climbers and stage-race specialists in with a chance of victory. The defining aspect of its route is the succession of sharp climbs through the Belgian Ardennes, including the iconic Côte de la Redoute, which make it arguably the most physically demanding Classic of all.

Epic edition

Often the victim of treacherous weather, Liège-Bastogne-Liège never took place in worse conditions than in 1980, when snow fell from the start and temperatures stayed close to freezing. Bernard Hinault won with 10 minutes to spare after attacking with 80km left, but at a cost. The great Frenchman lost movement in two fingers in his right hand for three weeks afterwards and feels numbness in them to this day.

Bear cheek

Irishman Dan Martin edged out Joaquim Rodríguez, of Spain, in 2013 to win one of the most thrilling finishes of recent years, but he was actually followed over the line by a man running in a panda suit. The unlikely spectacle led to a partnership between Martin's Garmin-Sharp team and the World Wildlife Fund.

'It is the most beautiful Classic on the calendar. It's the only race where you can be certain that the riders on the podium are the strongest. In other races, being clever can make up for a lack of strength, but not Liège.'

Michele Bartoli (Ita), winner 1997 & 1998

KEY CLIMBS ☞

0   20   40   60   80   100   120

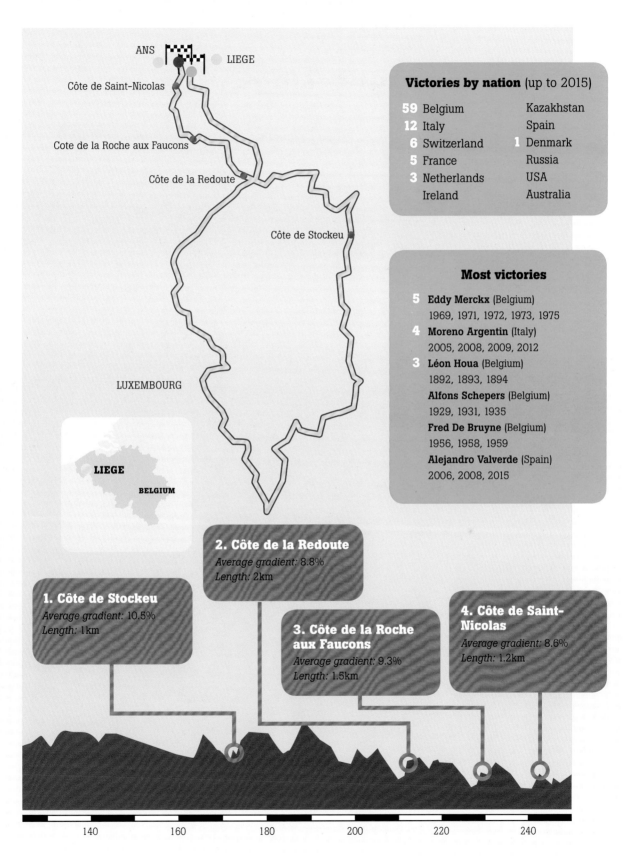

ANS

LIEGE

Côte de Saint-Nicolas

Cote de la Roche aux Faucons

Côte de la Redoute

Côte de Stockeu

LUXEMBOURG

LIEGE

BELGIUM

Most victories

5 **Eddy Merckx** (Belgium)
1969, 1971, 1972, 1973, 1975

4 **Moreno Argentin** (Italy)
2005, 2008, 2009, 2012

3 **Léon Houa** (Belgium)
1892, 1893, 1894

Alfons Schepers (Belgium)
1929, 1931, 1935

Fred De Bruyne (Belgium)
1956, 1958, 1959

Alejandro Valverde (Spain)
2006, 2008, 2015

2. Côte de la Redoute
Average gradient: 8.8%
Length: 2km

1. Côte de Stockeu
Average gradient: 10.5%
Length: 1km

3. Côte de la Roche aux Faucons
Average gradient: 9.3%
Length: 1.5km

4. Côte de Saint-Nicolas
Average gradient: 8.6%
Length: 1.2km

140   160   180   200   220   240

Earning power

Professional cyclists on the UCI Tour will spend around 220 days a year away from home, training for months on end while sharing hotel rooms with team-mates rather than wives and girlfriends. They will spend about 80 days of the year racing and cover about 10,000km in competition, racing in all manner of weather conditions and at serious risk of injury, but the financial rewards surely make up for it…

£4m

Chris Froome's reported salary for 2016 with Team Sky, a £1 million increase on his previous year's wages. In 2015, his main rivals Nairo Quintana and Alberto Contador were on similar wages to Froome at the time. Vincenzo Nibali, winner of the 2014 Tour, was said to be on £2.25-£2.5m.

£1m

Bradley Wiggins's bonus from Team Sky for winning the 2012 Tour. Team etiquette demanded that he shared the windfall with team-mates, but Wiggins withheld payments to Chris Froome for 14 months as a result of the tension between the pair, which boiled over when Froome raced away from Wiggins during the Tour despite supposedly serving as his domestique. Froome received the payments only after team principal Dave Brailsford intervened.

$1m

The American legend Greg Lemond helped to lift elite cyclists' earnings to a new level in the 1980s, signing the first million-dollar contract in 1985 and then, in 1989, clinching a deal worth $5.5million over three years with the French team Z-Tomasso. At the time, it was the richest contract ever given to a rider.

includes figures published by sky sports

POCKET MONEY

Cyclists were not always paid well. **Roger Walkowiak** was riding a la musette for the St Raphaël-Géminiani trade squad when he won the 1956 Tour de France. This meant the Frenchman got a bike, racing kit and precious little else but modest winning bonuses. His earnings did dramatically increase as a result of his victory, though.

£8,000,000

Mark Cavendish's estimated net worth, taking into account earnings, prize money and sponsorship.

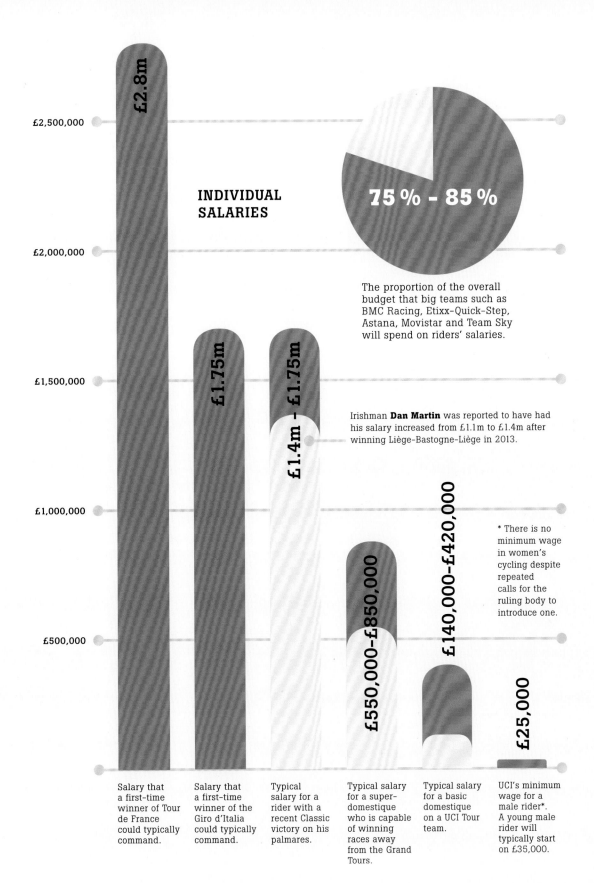

£2,500,000

£2.8m

INDIVIDUAL
SALARIES

75 % – 85 %

The proportion of the overall
budget that big teams such as
BMC Racing, Etixx-Quick-Step,
Astana, Movistar and Team Sky
will spend on riders' salaries.

£2,000,000

£1,500,000

£1.75m

£1.75m

£1.4m – £1.75m

Irishman **Dan Martin** was reported to have had
his salary increased from £1.1m to £1.4m after
winning Liège-Bastogne-Liège in 2013.

£1,000,000

£140,000–£420,000

* There is no
minimum wage
in women's
cycling despite
repeated
calls for the
ruling body to
introduce one.

£550,000–£850,000

£500,000

£25,000

Salary that
a first-time
winner of Tour
de France
could typically
command.

Salary that
a first-time
winner of the
Giro d'Italia
could typically
command.

Typical
salary for a
rider with a
recent Classic
victory on his
palmares.

Typical salary
for a super-
domestique
who is capable
of winning
races away
from the Grand
Tours.

Typical salary
for a basic
domestique
on a UCI Tour
team.

UCI's minimum
wage for a
male rider*.
A young male
rider will
typically start
on £35,000.

Visions of glory

From John Lennon-style lenses to movie-star shades, and military-style spectacles, the professional peloton has seen some memorable pairs of glasses.

MILITARY CHIC

Ottavio Bottecchia
The first Italian to win the Tour de France, in 1925, was typical of riders from his generation in that he wore military-grade flying goggles to protect himself from the dust, the occasional flying insect and bits of debris that flew up from the mostly unpaved roads. In the early days, the googles were made from leather and glass, though rubber eventually replaced the former as it was lighter.

SHADES OF SUCCESS

Fausto Coppi
The military-style googles remained de rigueur among the professional peloton until the 1950s, when Coppi was among the first to wear sunglasses, which film stars of the era had made popular. The most commonly used brands were Persol and Ray-Ban, with Coppi choosing a pair of the latter's signature Aviator shades, adding Hollywood cool to his already iconic status.

LOOKING SLICK

Jan Janssen
The first Dutchman to win the Tour, in 1968, was one of the first champions to wear conventional glasses, to cure his myopia. He chose fashionable thick-rimmed frames, which fitted his status as one of the most stylish riders. Out of the saddle, he had slicked-back blond hair, wore a tailored suit travelling to races and carried equipment in a leather suitcase rather than a gym bag.

BLURRED VISION

Laurent Fignon
Two-time Tour winner Fignon admitted to mixed feelings about the John Lennon-style round glasses with which he was associated. While he liked that they contributed – along with his pigtail and blond hair – to an idiosyncratic image that ensured he stood out from the rest, they were also a hindrance at a time before contact lenses were popular because the lenses collected mud and water.

A NEW FOCUS

Greg LeMond
Triple Tour champion LeMond helped to pioneer cycling-specific glasses when, along with the Australian Phil Anderson, he wore a pair of Oakleys at the 1985 Tour. Created by the American designer Jim Jannard, who started out in the BMX market and named the company after his dog Oakley, the 'eyeshades' were large, colourful and robust, being made out of a new plastic called Zytel.

CLEAN VIEW

Alex Zulle
Oakley were among the first brands to produce the curved prescription lens more suited to cycling, which meant that short-sighted competitors such as Alex Zulle – twice a winner of the Vuelta a España in the 1990s – no longer had to suffer from dry eyes brought about by hours spent wearing contact lenses in the heat. The Swiss rider was synonymous with his pair of distinctive Rudy Project shades.

ICON Sir Bradley Wiggins

National icon, counter-culture hero, Olympic legend and Tour de France champion, Wiggins enjoyed an unusually varied career for an elite rider. Born in Belgium to an English mother and Australian father, but raised on a London council estate, his background was far from the typical one for an aspiring professional cyclist, especially as he grew up when the sport was still a minority concern in Britain. Yet he defied his upbringing to excel, firstly, on the track and then the road, helping to inspire a generation of internationally successful British riders and to amplify the sport's popularity in his country.

8

Wiggins became Britain's most decorated Olympian ever at Rio 2016, winning his eighth medal in total, and fifth gold as part of the British quartet who won the team pursuit.

2012

Wiggins's golden year as he became the first Briton to win the Tour de France and won the Olympic time trial, earning him a knighthood and the BBC Sports Personality of the Year award.

THE FACTS

Full name **Bradley Marc Wiggins**

Nickname **Wiggo**

Date of birth **April 28, 1980**

Birthplace **Ghent, Flanders**

Height **6ft 3in (1.90m)**

'Right, we're just going to draw the raffle numbers... Some dreams do come true. My old mother over there, her son has just won the Tour de France... Thanks again. Have a safe journey home. Don't get too drunk.'

Wiggins on the podium after the 2012 Tour de France

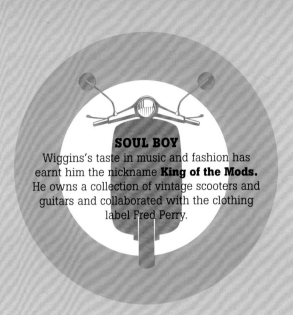

SOUL BOY
Wiggins's taste in music and fashion has earnt him the nickname **King of the Mods.** He owns a collection of vintage scooters and guitars and collaborated with the clothing label Fred Perry.

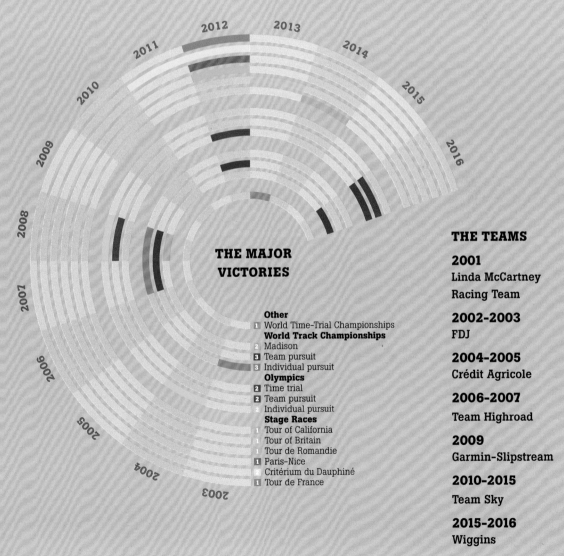

THE MAJOR VICTORIES

Other
1 World Time-Trial Championships
World Track Championships
2 Madison
3 Team pursuit
3 Individual pursuit
Olympics
2 Time trial
2 Team pursuit
2 Individual pursuit
Stage Races
1 Tour of California
1 Tour of Britain
1 Tour de Romandie
1 Paris-Nice
1 Critérium du Dauphiné
1 Tour de France

THE TEAMS

2001
Linda McCartney
Racing Team

2002-2003
FDJ

2004-2005
Crédit Agricole

2006-2007
Team Highroad

2009
Garmin-Slipstream

2010-2015
Team Sky

2015-2016
Wiggins

Who runs what

While the UCI is cycling's global ruling body, they delegate some power to the five continental federations, who in turn oversee the individual, national federations. At the last count, there were 173 affiliated national federations. The president of each continental body, meanwhile, is given a seat on the UCI management committee that makes the final decisions on the sport.

British Cycling
The national governing body for the sport in Britain is an example of one of the national federations. Clubs affiliate to it to race in BC events, across a variety of disciplines. BC represents national interests at the UCI and selects national teams, including the Olympic team.

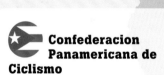

Confederacion Panamericana de Ciclismo
Based: Havana
President: José Manuel Peláez Rodríguez (Cuba)
Member nations: 42

Confederation Africaine de Cyclisme
Based: Cairo
President: Dr Mohamed Wagih Azzam (Egypt)
Member nations: 37

Union Cycliste Internationale

Role: Global ruling body
Founded: 1900
Based: Aigle, near Lausanne, Switzerland
HQ: Offices, library, velodrome, training centre
Owns: World Championships
Key responsibilities: Grants racing licences, leads anti-doping agenda, runs disciplinary cases, decides on equipment regulations, maintains the World Tour.

Union Européenne de Cyclisme

Based: Lausanne
President: David Lappartient (France)
Member nations: 48

POWER STRUGGLE

In 2014, a supergroup of 11 World Tour teams, including Team Sky and Tinkoff-Saxo, formed Velon. Their aim was to reduce the reliance on sponsors and make the sport more entertaining.

The French teams did not get involved, it is thought out of loyalty to the influential Amaury Sports Organisation, which owns the Tour de France and Vuelta a España among other races.

In November 2015, the Paris-based ASO withdrew the Tour from the World Tour in protest at UCI reforms, which included an extended calendar and longer team licences.

ASO felt their power was threatened by the changes and by Velon. This battle is set to rumble on.

Asian Cycling Confederation

Based: Seoul
President: Cho Hee-Wok (South Korea)
Member nations: 39

Oceania Cycling Confederation

Based: Adelaide
President: Tracey Gaudry (Australia)
Member nations: 6

The individual pursuit

One of the most compelling track-cycling disciplines, the individual pursuit is a contest between two riders who begin on opposites side of the track and attempt to complete the distance in the quickest time. In especially one-sided races, the stronger rider can also win by catching his opponent before the full distance has been run.

4 km

Length of the men's race. Sixteen laps of an Olympic track.

3 km
Length of the women's race. Twelve laps of an Olympic track.

3

Great Britain's three Olympic titles in the men's event is the most of any country. Chris Boardman won it in 1992. Sir Bradley Wiggins triumphed in 2004 and 2008.

Olympic rejection

The men's individual pursuit was included at the Olympics from 1964 until 2008. The women's version ran from 1992 to 2008, after which the UCI dropped both versions to concentrate on endurance events. Britain's Olympic legend Sir Chris Hoy described the decision as 'frustrating for the entire cycling community'.

World history

There has been an individual pursuit for men at the World Championships since being introduced to them in 1946. There was both an amateur and professional race until 1991, when the two classes were amalgamated.

Women have contested the event at all but one Worlds since its first inclusion in 1958. It was omitted in Valencia in 1992 when women contested only one discipline, the points race.

14

The 14 professional world titles won by Great Britain's men is the most of any nation.
Hugh Porter 1968, 1970, 1972, 1973,
Tony Doyle 1980, 1986
Colin Sturgess 1989
Graeme Obree 1993, 1995
Chris Boardman 1994, 1996
Sir Bradley Wiggins 2003, 2007, 2008

6

Two women share the record of six world titles.
Tamara Garkuchina (USSR) 1967, 1970, 1971, 1972, 1973, 1974,
Rebecca Twigg (USA) 1982, 1984, 1985, 1987, 1993, 1995

PROGRESSION OF WORLD RECORD

Men

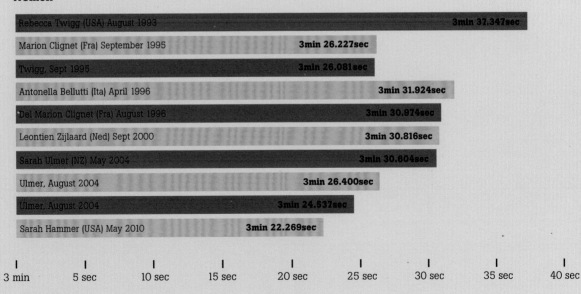

Philippe Ermenault (Fra) July 1993	4min 23.562sec
Ermenault, August 1993	4min 23.283sec
Graeme Obree (GB) August 1993	4min 22.668sec
Obree, August 1993	4min 20.894sec
Andrea Collinelli (Ita) July 1996	4min 19.699sec
Chris Boardman (GB) August 1996	4min 13.353sec
Boardman, August 1996	4min 11.114sec
Jack Bobridge (Aus) February 2011	4min 10.534sec

4 min   5 sec   10 sec   15 sec   20 sec   25 sec

Women

Rebecca Twigg (USA) August 1993	3min 37.347sec
Marion Clignet (Fra) September 1995	3min 26.227sec
Twigg, Sept 1995	3min 26.081sec
Antonella Bellutti (Ita) April 1996	3min 31.924sec
Del Marion Clignet (Fra) August 1996	3min 30.974sec
Leontien Zijlaard (Ned) Sept 2000	3min 30.816sec
Sarah Ulmer (NZ) May 2004	3min 30.604sec
Ulmer, August 2004	3min 26.400sec
Ulmer, August 2004	3min 24.537sec
Sarah Hammer (USA) May 2010	3min 22.269sec

3 min   5 sec   10 sec   15 sec   20 sec   25 sec   30 sec   35 sec   40 sec

'The devil in a dress'

In 1924, long before women had their own versions of the Grand Tours, Alfonsina Strada became the only woman ever to ride one of the men's three editions when she completed the Giro d'Italia. Initially derided in a fiercely masculine world, she went on to win over thousands of fans with her effort.

THE FACTS

Born **March 16, 1891**

Birthplace **Castelfranco Emilia, Modena**

Height **5ft 2in**

Nickname **Locals were said to have crossed the street when they saw the tomboy Strada riding her bike, thinking she was marked by Satan, while newspapers called her 'the devil in a dress'.**

10
Her father, having seen her love for the sport, acquired Strada's first bicycle in exchange for chickens when she was aged 10.

13
She won her first race aged 13, winning a live pig.

20
Strada was only 20 when she set the women's hour record of 37.192km in Moncalieri, near Turin.

36
The number of races she won against men.

2
She twice rode the Tour of Lombardy when it was open to men and women, finishing 32nd and last in 1917, but ahead of several men when she came 21st a year later.

The historic 1924 Giro

1 She enters as Alfonsin Strada after the officials opened the race to all-comers. That she is a woman only emerges the day before the start in Milan, by which time it is too late to force her withdrawal.

2 One of 90 riders to begin the race, Strada finishes the first stage in Genoa in 74th place. It is one of eight mountain stages in the 12-stage race.

3 She is 50th out of 64 riders still in the race by the end of the fourth stage in Naples.

6 She finishes 36th out of the 38 riders to make it to the end of the 3,613km course and wins 50,000 lire, which was raised by public donations.

5 Crying with exhaustion at the end of stage 10 into Fiume, she is lifted from her bicycle in triumph by fans and carried shoulder-high, giving her the motivation to continue.

4 She finishes outside the time limit on the seventh stage after crashing badly on a descent. However, officials bow to public pressure asking her to be allowed to continue. She raced on as an individual.

Verona
Fiume
Milano
Genoa
Bologna
Firenze
Perugia
L'Aquila
Roma
Foggia
Napoli
Taranto

159

Pedal pushers

You could write a short book on how racing cyclists' shoes have developed over the decades, such has been their transformation. Here is a selection of the seminal designs.

Vintage cut

With laced, black leather uppers and wooden soles, the cycling shoes used in the decades after World War II were far heavier than their modern version but they still look stylish now.

Anyone wishing to attempt the retro-look should match them with white socks, as was de rigueur at the time.

Fresh sole

Dino Signori, a former Italian junior rider who had set up his own shoe-making company, transformed the design of cycling shoes in 1973 with a pair that had adjustable cleats when previously they had been nailed on. Signori's company, SIDI, remains a market-leader in the field partly as a result of the breakthrough.

Control stick

The Velcro strap closures that were introduced in 1983 quickly became popular because they made for a more secure fit than the traditional, laced footwear and were easier to adjust during a race.

Step change

For decades, riders wore shoes fitted with slotted metal shoe plates that clipped on to the pedal and were then secured with the aid of metal toe straps and leather straps. However, in 1984, ski equipment manufacturer Look produced pedals from which cyclists could release their foot by twisting it sideways, eliminating the need for the metal toe clips. Some professionals were skeptical until Bernard Hinault won the 1985 Tour de France using them.

Screw fix

With a microfibre upper and carbon sole, the top-of-the-range modern shoe is considerably lighter than its predecessors. Riders can choose from a range of closure systems too, from Velcro to buckles and ratchets, though a new style has quickly become popular among the peloton. Developed by a Denver-based company, Boa Technology tightens shoes using a series of dials to dissipate the friction placed on the foot.

The rollercoaster life of Richard Virenque

Emotional, courageous and good-looking, Frenchman Richard Virenque went from national icon to pariah when he admitted to doping after years of denial. And it was only the first of several dramatic events in one of the most tumultuous cycling careers.

Born to an affluent family in the wealthy Iseba district of Casablanca. They employ a gardener and nurse.

Competes in his first Tour de France and takes the yellow jersey on day three after a successful breakaway. He eventually finishes second in the climbers' competition.

The UCI forces the Tour to re-admit Virenque into the race. His links to doping and his divisive personality have made him unpopular with many fans and riders, prompting him to travel between stages with a bodyguard.

After racing throughout his teenage years, the Frenchman finishes eighth in the amateur world road race. The feat earns him his first professional contract.

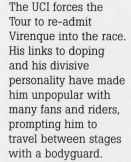

HAPPINESS

SADNESS

Virenque starts cycling but struggles at school. 'I soon realised that I didn't have the brain to be anything but a racing cyclist,' he said.

The family move to the south of France but his parents' relationship breaks down and they divorce. 'It was a difficult moment,' Virenque said. 'I had only my bike and I took to it in depth.'

A doping network is exposed within Virenque's Festina team. Several team-mates are disqualified after admitting to using EPO, but Virenque insists on his innocence.

Virenque is banned from the 1999 Tour after his name emerges in an inquiry into Bernard Sainz, aka 'Dr Mabuse', who was jailed for practising as an unqualified doctor and was found with performance-enhancing drugs in his car.

| 1969 | 1977 | 1979 | 1990 | 1992 | 1998 | 1999 | 1999 |

Publishes his book *Ma Verite* in which he reasserts his innocence and insists that doping must be fought. He also says team-mates admitted to using EPO only because of pressure from the police.

Returns from his doping ban to join the Domo-Farm Frites team after most other squads shun him.

Wins a record seventh polka-dot jersey at the Tour. Retires at the end of the season.

Wins the French version of the reality TV show *I'm A Celebrity Get Me Out Of Here*.

Starts dating Jessica Sow, a model 19 years younger than him.

He admits to doping at a trial into the Festina Affair, but claims he did not do it intentionally, blaming team staff for giving him products that he did not realise were banned.

Is widely ridiculed after telling a TV interview that he would dope again if he knew that it would win him the Tour and he would not get caught.

The satirical French TV show *Les Guignols* (The Puppets) produces a moronic rubber puppet of Virenque with hypodermic needles stuck in its head. Its catchprase *'à l'insu de mon plein gré'* ('willingly but without knowing') passes into French popular culture as a hypocritical denial.

Divorces his wife Stéphanie after 17 years of marriage. They had two children.

1999   2000   2000   2001   2001   2004   2006   2007   2008

Cycling at the Olympics

The sport has been included at every modern Games since the first one in Athens in 1896.

The first Games

In 1896, six track events – the sprint, time trial, individual pursuit, 10km, 100km and 12-hour race – and a road race were included at the first modern Games in Athens. They were all for men.

Low point

The United States team admitted that they used systematic (but, at the time, legal) blood doping en route to winning nine medals in 1984. The practice was banned the following January.

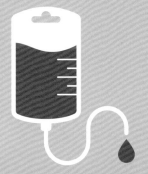

A step forward

The Games included its first women's event in 1984 when the road race was held in Los Angeles. Women were given track events for the first time four years later in Seoul.

Great Britons

GB dominated the 2008 Games like no nation had ever done, winning eight golds and 14 medals in total. They matched the gold-haul four years later, when they won a total of 12 medals. They won the same number of medals in 2016, with six golds.

Equality at last

The London Games of 2012 was the first in which the same number of cycling events were held for men and women. Previously, there had always been fewer for women.

MOST DECORATED OLYMPIANS

Men

= Chris Hoy (GB)
Games 2000, 2004, 2008, 2012

WWWW 6

V 1

= Jason Kenny (GB)
Games 2008, 2012, 2016

WWWW 6

V 1

Bradley Wiggins (GB)
Games 2000, 2004, 2008, 2012

WWW 4

V 1

WW 2

Women

Leontien Van Moorsel (Ned)
Games 2000, 2002, 2004

WWW 4

V 1

V 1

Félicia Ballanger (Fra)
Games 1996, 2000

WW 3

Anna Meares (Aus)
Games 2004, 2008, 2012

W 2

V 1

WW 2

ALL-TIME MEDAL TABLE

1. France

WWWWWWWWWWWWWWWWWWWWW 41

WWWWWWWWWWWWWW 27

WWWWWWWWWWWW 23

2. Great Britain

WWWWWWWWWWWWWWWW 32

WWWWWWWWWWWWWWW 30

WWWWWWWWWWW 25

3. Italy

WWWWWWWWWWWWWWWW 32

WWWWWWWW 16

WWWWW 9

4. Netherlands

WWWWWWWWW 18

WWWWWWWWW 18

WWWWWW 12

5. United States

WWWWWWWW 15

WWWWWWWWWW 20

WWWWWWWWWW 20

*Statistics do not include the BMX and mountain-bike competitions at the 2016 Games

Monument #5
Tour of Lombardy

'The Race of the Falling Leaves'
First edition: 1905
Distance: 242km (2016)

The final Monument of the year is the most visually impressive one-day race because of its setting amid the snow-capped peaks around Lake Como and the scene created by the autumn leaves that settle on the route's lower roads. It is also often the site for thrilling competition as it combines tough climbs with a long sprint finish. The golden age of the race ran from the 1920s through to the 1950s when the exploits of the great Italian riders Alfredo Binda, Fausto Coppi and Gino Bartali earnt it an elevated status on the calendar. For the modern fan, however, it is more closely associated with the Madonna del Ghisallo chapel that sits on its decisive climb and is a site of pilgrimage for every cycle-racing devotee, filled as it is with cycling memorabilia.

Most victories

5 **Fausto Coppi** (Italy; *above*)
1946, 1947, 1948, 1949, 1954

4 **Alfredo Binda** (Italy)
1925, 1926, 1927, 1931

3 **Henri Pélissier** (France)
1911, 1913, 1920

3 **Costante Girardengo** (Italy)
1919, 1921, 1922

3 **Gaetano Belloni** (Italy)
1915, 1918, 1928

3 **Gino Bartali** (Italy)
1936, 1939, 1940

3 **Sean Kelly** (Ireland)
1983 1985, 1991

Godly pursuit
In a sport closely linked to Catholicism, the best known of the several cyclists' chapels in Europe is the Madonna del Ghisallo on the climb from Lake Como. A statue of Fausto Coppi stands outside it while inside are bikes and jerseys donated by many of the sport's most celebrated riders.

34
Number of raw eggs that Alfredo Binda ate en route to winning his fourth Tour of Lombardy in 1931 by 18 minutes from second-placed Michele Mara (Ita). Incessant rain meant all other food dissolved in his pocket.

1. Colle Gallo
Average gradient: 6%
Maximum gradient: 10%
Length: 7.4km

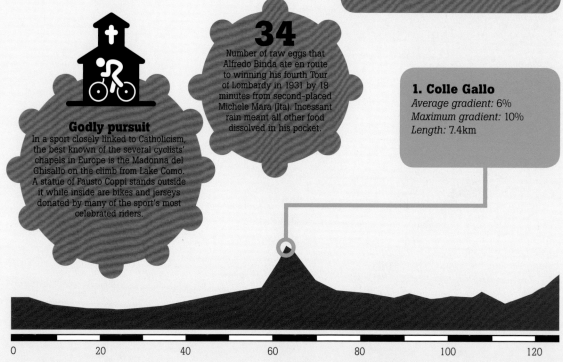

0   20   40   60   80   100   120

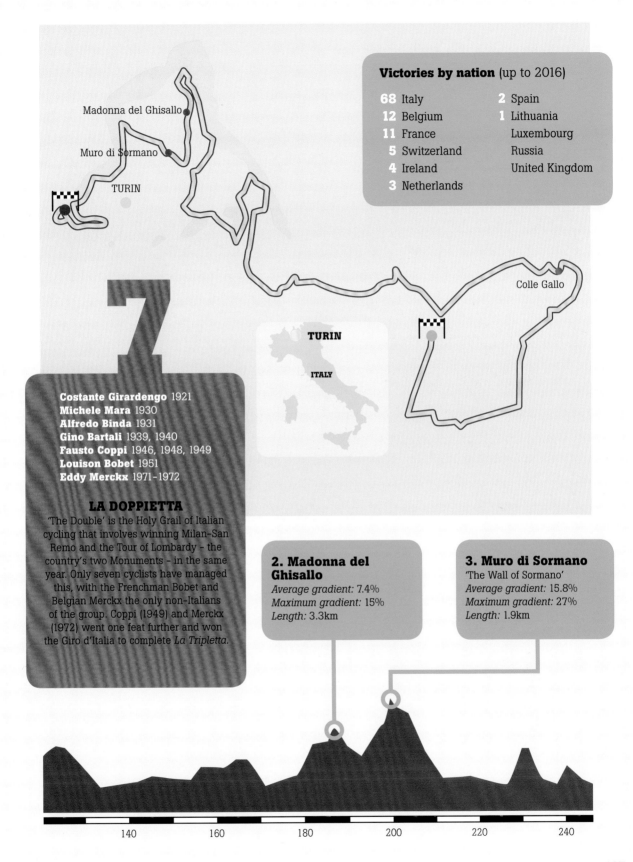

Victories by nation (up to 2016)

68	Italy	**2**	Spain
12	Belgium	**1**	Lithuania
11	France		Luxembourg
5	Switzerland		Russia
4	Ireland		United Kingdom
3	Netherlands		

Madonna del Ghisallo

Muro di Sormano

TURIN

Colle Gallo

TURIN

ITALY

7

Costante Girardengo 1921
Michele Mara 1930
Alfredo Binda 1931
Gino Bartali 1939, 1940
Fausto Coppi 1946, 1948, 1949
Louison Bobet 1951
Eddy Merckx 1971–1972

LA DOPPIETTA

'The Double' is the Holy Grail of Italian cycling that involves winning Milan-San Remo and the Tour of Lombardy – the country's two Monuments – in the same year. Only seven cyclists have managed this, with the Frenchman Bobet and Belgian Merckx the only non-Italians of the group. Coppi (1949) and Merckx (1972) went one feat further and won the Giro d'Italia to complete *La Tripletta*.

2. Madonna del Ghisallo
Average gradient: 7.4%
Maximum gradient: 15%
Length: 3.3km

3. Muro di Sormano
'The Wall of Sormano'
Average gradient: 15.8%
Maximum gradient: 27%
Length: 1.9km

140   160   180   200   220   240

ICON Marianne Vos

A winner of the Olympic road race, World Champion on the track and the most successful ever cyclo-cross rider, Marianne Vos is a rider of exceptional talent and versatility. She competed in her first race aged eight and went on to dominate the Dutch junior scene before becoming the first woman ever to hold world titles on the road, track and in cyclo-cross, when she was 21. Since then she has established herself, to quote Eddy Merckx, as 'the finest cyclist of her generation'. In truth, she is one of the very best of all time.

What she said

'It can be boring. I ask myself: "If you win over and over again, do you get the Lance Armstrong effect?" I don't want that. But I also don't want to lose races because it's boring for the spectators. I don't want to harm women's cycling because of my winning, but I don't want to half do things.'

20

Number of stage victories at the Giro d'Italia

ULTIMATE ACCOLADE

In Italy, they gave Vos the same nickname as the great Eddy Merckx, 'The Cannibal', such was her appetite for victory.

THE FACTS

Full name **Marianne Vos**

Nickname **The Cannibal**

Date of birth **May 13, 1987**

Birthplace **'s-Hertogenbosch, Netherlands**

Team **DSB-Ballast Nedam, 2006–**

Height **5ft 6in (1.68m)**

THE MAJOR VICTORIES

	2006	2007	2008	2009	2010	2011	2012	2013	2014
GIRO D'ITALIA FEMMINILE									
General classification						●	●		●
Points classification		●			●	●	●	●	●
Mountains classification						●			
OTHER STAGE RACES									
Emakumeen Bira			●			●			
Holland Ladies Tour				●	●		●		
The Women's Tour (GB)									●
Grand Prix Elsy Jacobs							●	●	
WORLD TITLES									
Road race	●						●	●	
Cyclo-cross	●			●	●	●		●	●
Points race			●						
Scratch race						●			
OLYMPIC GAMES									
Points race			●						
Road race							●		
UCI WOMEN'S ROAD WORLD CUP									
Overall winner		●		●	●		●	●	
GP CIUDAD DE VALLADOLID						●			
GP DE PLOUAY						●			
LA FLÈCHE WALLONNE FÉMININE		●							
TOUR OF FLANDERS FOR WOMEN								●	
OPEN DE SUEDE VARGARDA				●				●	
RONDE VAN DRENTHE						●	●	●	
RUN UM DIE NUMBERGER ALTSTADT		●							
TROFEO ALFREDO BINDA				●	●		●		
SPARKASSEN GIRO BOCHUM									●

*Statistics correct up to and including 2015.

PROTEST LEADER

Vos teamed up with fellow high-profile female riders Emma Pooley, Kathryn Bertine, and Chrissie Wellington to persuade the organisers of the Tour de France to allow women to race at the event. Their petition attracted almost 100,000 signatures and led to the formation of La Course by Le Tour, a one-day race on the final day of the men's Tour. Vos, naturally, won its first edition in 2014.

Secrets of the soigneurs

As a confidante, masseur and a tactical advisor, the soigneur has played a wide-ranging role in the careers of many great cyclists – not least because these support staff were also often the source of their clients' drugs. Here are six whose contribution to the sport has been among the most memorable of all.

BIAGIO CAVANNA
Italy

The blind Italian masseur who most famously worked with all-time greats **Costante Girardengo** and **Fausto Coppi** earned an almost mythical status for his emotional insight and healing power.

What he said:

'My hands see more than my eyes. My ears hear what can't be heard.'

What they said:

'He could go inside the mind of the athlete and indicate to each guy how they should prepare.'

Alfredo Martini, former Italian cyclist and a team-mate of Coppi's.

JULIEN SCHRAMM
France

One of the most prominent soigneurs of the 1950s, Schramm was best known for his long-standing relationship with **Jacques Anquetil**, the great French cyclist.

What he said:

Schramm claimed the 50 ampoules of Tonedrone, an amphetamine, which were found on his person were for his own use. However, he refused to prove it by injecting himself with it.

What Anquetil said:

'I used to drink about four or five pints of milk a day, but since Julien told me that it was toxic I drink beer instead.'

GUS NAESSENS
Belgium

Among the best-paid soigneurs in the 1960s, Naessens included **Tom Simpson** among his clients and was working with the Briton when Simpson died on Mont Ventoux with ampethamines in his system.

What he said:

It was widely reported that Naessens boiled cattle feed into porridge and put it in cyclist's bottles in the belief it would sit in the stomach, telling the riders it would help them to store energy.

What they said:

Simpson told reporters that Naessens was crucial to his victory in Paris-Nice in 1967.

GUILLAUME MICHIELS
Belgium

After a moderate racing career in the late 1950s and '60s, the Belgian Michiels earned far more renown as **Eddy Merckx's** career-long soigneur and close confidante.

What he said (about Merckx):
'We know everything about each other. The things that are not known by others and the things that will never be known by others.'

What Merckx said:
'He is my second brother.'

WILLY VOET
Belgium

The Belgian physiotherapist was notorious for being rumbled by police in 1998 with a car-load of drugs while driving to the Tour de France as soigneur to the Festina team.

What he said (in 1999):
'In my opinion, 90% of the peloton is using banned substances at the moment.'

What they said:
'Voet's inside view of the ways of cycling leading up to the Festina scandal remains vitally important to understand the pressures which lead sportsmen to take drugs.'

William Fotheringham, the English translator of Voet's autobiography.

EMMA O'REILLY
Ireland

Female soigneurs helped to dispel the mystical aura that surrounded the work of the soigneur when they began to find work on the men's Tour in the late 1980s. O'Reilly became the most high-profile when she tried to blow the whistle on **Lance Armstrong**, having worked with the American on the US Postal Team. (O'Reilly herself was never implicated in helping him to dope.)

What she said:
'People say they are amazed I forgave Lance, but from being on the inside I think he had to forgive me too because I did spit in the soup and break the omerta.'

What Armstrong said (about his treatment of O'Reilly):
'It was inexcusable. If I saw my son do that, there would be a f------ war in our house.'

Armstrong had called O'Reilly an 'alcoholic whore' when she first accused him of doping.

Kings of the world

The men's annual World Road Race Championships is the most prestigious one-day race in the calendar. It takes place towards the end of the season, usually after the Vuelta a España. For decades after its inception in 1921, there was a title race for amateurs and a separate one for professionals, but the two were amalgamated into a single event in 1995. In the worlds, they compete with their national team rather than their sponsored one, but the only prize is for individuals, with the winner being given the world champion's coveted rainbow jersey. Our chart lists the event's most successful participants.

Rider	Years with marks (1921–1960)
Alfredo Binda	1927, 1930, 1932
Rik Van Steenbergen	1949, 1956, 1957
Oscar Freire	—
Eddy Merckx	—
Rik Van Looy	1956, 1960
Greg LeMond	—
Freddy Maertens	—
Paolo Bettini	—
Georges Ronsse	1928, 1929, 1930
Gianni Bugno	—
Briek Schotte	1948, 1950
Learco Guerra	1930, 1931, 1934
Francesco Moser	—
André Darrigade	1957, 1958, 1959, 1960
Theo Middelkamp	1947
Ferdi Kübler	1948, 1949, 1950
Felice Gimondi	—
Giuseppe Saronni	—
Moreno Argentin	—
Jan Janssen	—
Rudi Altig	—
Vittorio Adorni	—

Year axis: 1921 1922 1923 1924 1925 1926 1927 1928 1929 1930 1931 1932 1933 1934 1935 1936 1937 1938 1939 1940 1941 1942 1943 1944 1945 1946 1947 1948 1949 1950 1951 1952 1953 1954 1955 1956 1957 1958 1959 1960

Figures correct up to 2015.

5

Only five riders have successfully defended their title. The Belgians Georges Ronsse, Rik Van Steenbergen and Rik Van Looy, and the Italian pair Gianni Bugno and Paolo Bettini.

6

Alejandro Valverde has won more medals in the event, with six, more than any other rider though he has never won it. The Spaniard has two silvers (2003, 2005) and four bronzes (2006, 2010-12).

26

Belgium's 26 victories in the competition is more than any other country, with Italy's 19 placing them second. Italian riders, though, have won the most medals in total, with 55, ahead of 48 for Belgians.

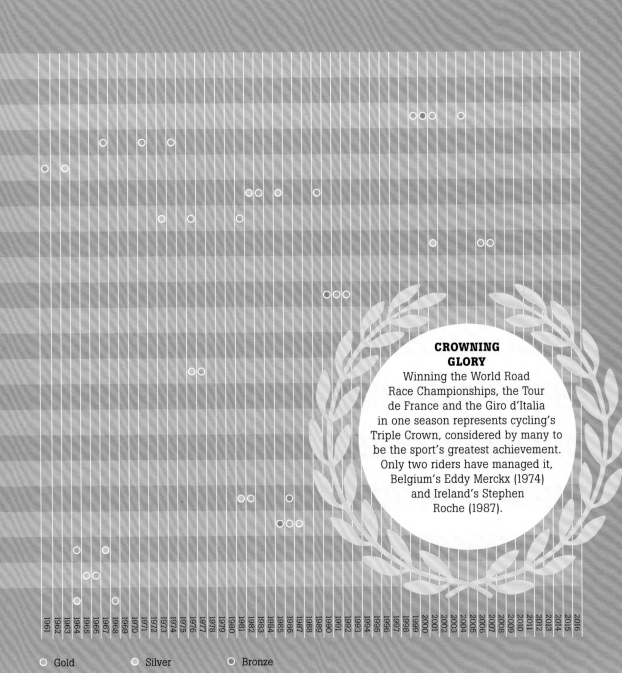

CROWNING GLORY

Winning the World Road Race Championships, the Tour de France and the Giro d'Italia in one season represents cycling's Triple Crown, considered by many to be the sport's greatest achievement. Only two riders have managed it, Belgium's Eddy Merckx (1974) and Ireland's Stephen Roche (1987).

○ Gold   ○ Silver   ○ Bronze

ICON Mark Cavendish

Put simply, the best road sprinter who has ever lived. Though schooled on the track through the British Cycling academy system, Cavendish has enjoyed one of the most successful careers of all since switching to the road, posting the second-most stage wins (and counting) at the Tour de France, the points classification at every Grand Tour and 48 Grand Tour stages in total, the joint-third most in history. After what, for the Manxman, was a dip in success during 2014 and 2015, he banished all suggestions that he might have lost his speed in 2016 by winning four stages at the Tour despite quitting the race early to allow him to compete at the Rio Olympics – where he won his first ever medal at a Games by claiming silver in the omnium.

What he said

'It doesn't matter whether it's raining or the sun is shining or whatever: as long as I'm riding a bike I know I'm the luckiest guy in the world.'

THE FACTS

Full name **Mark Simon Cavendish**

Nickname **The Manx Missile**

Date of birth **May 21, 1985**

Birthplace **Douglas, Isle of Man**

Height **5ft 9in (1.75m)**

THE RECORD BREAKER

2005
■ Won the first of his three world titles on the track, triumphing in the madison with Rob Hayles.

2007
■ Equalled Alessandro Petacchi's (Ita) record of 11 wins in first season as a professional.

2009
■ Became the second Briton — after Tom Simpson — to win one of the five Monuments with victory in Milan-San Remo.
■ Became first British rider to wear the leader's jersey at the Giro d'Italia.

2010
■ Became the second Briton — after Robert Millar — to win a stage in all three Grand Tours with victory on stage 12 of the Vuelta. He went on to win the points classification in the race, his first in a Grand Tour.

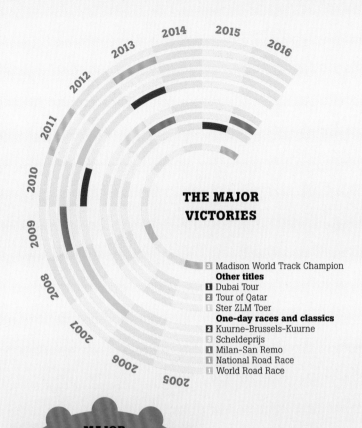

**THE MAJOR
VICTORIES**

3 Madison World Track Champion
Other titles
1 Dubai Tour
2 Tour of Qatar
1 Ster ZLM Toer
One-day races and classics
2 Kuurne-Brussels-Kuurne
3 Scheldeprijs
1 Milan-San Remo
1 National Road Race
1 World Road Race

THE TEAMS

2005-2006
Team Sparkasse

2006-2011
T-Mobile Team

2012
Team Sky

2013-2015
Omega Pharma-
QuickStep

2016
Team Dimension Data

30

Cavendish's 30 Tour de France
stage wins puts him second on
the all-time list, four behind Eddy
Merckx. How they break down:

2008 - **4**	2013 - **2**
2009 - **6**	2014 - **0**
2010 - **5**	2015 - **1**
2011 - **5**	2016 - **4**
2012 - **3**	

**MAJOR
ACHIEVEMENTS**
Grand Tours

Tour de France
Points classification 2011
30 individual-stage wins

Giro d'Italia
Points classification 2013
15 individual-stage wins

Vuelta a España
Points classification 2010
3 individual-stage win
1 team time trial victory

JOB PAY-OFF
Cavendish worked in Barclays
bank as a teenager before
joining the British Cycling
academy after one of his first
coaches suggested it would
be good for his cycling career
if he had a taste of the real
world.

2011

2012

2013

2016

■ Became the first Briton to
win the points classification at
the Tour.
■ Became the second Briton
– after Simpson – to win the
World Road Race title.

■ Became the first rider to
win the final stage of the Tour
on the Champs-Élysées four
years in a row.
■ Won his 23rd Tour stage
victory – all of which were
massed-start, the most of any
rider in history.

■ 100 professional wins with
victory on stage 12 of the Giro.
■ Completed his set of Grand
Tour points classifications
wins at the Giro, making him
only the fifth rider to do so.

■ Moved ahead of Bernard
Hinault (Fra) into second place
on the list of riders with the
most stage victories at the
Tour after another four wins
gave him 30 in total.

Figures correct up to September 2016.

Tour de France prize pot

The Tour champion tends to win far more than his domestiques but tradition counteracts that by demanding that the winner shares his windfall with team-mates. Given that the very top riders are thought to command salaries of about £3million, they are unlikely to complain.

Position	Prize	Position	Prize
1.	£354,000 (€452,000)	16.	£1,181 (€1,500)
2.	£157,490 (€200,000)	17.	£1,023 (€1,300)
3.	£78,750 (€100,000)	18.	£945 (€1,200)
4.	£55,120 (€70,000)	19.	£787 (€1,000)
5.	£39,380 (€50,2000)	20.	£748 (€950)
6.	£18,100 (€23,000)	21.	£708 (€900)
7.	£9,056 (€11,500)	22.	£669 (€850)
8.	£5,985 (€7,600)	23.	£590 (€750)
9.	£3,542 (€4,500)	24.	£551 (€700)
10.	£2,991 (€3,800)	25.	£512 (€650)
11.	£2,362 (€3,000)	26-30.	£472 (€600)
12.	£2,125 (€2,700)	31-40.	£433 (€550)
13.	£1,968 (€2,500)	41-50.	£394 (€500)
14.	£1,653 (€2,100)	51-90.	£354 (€450)
15.	£1,574 (€2,000)	90-159.	£315 (€400)

£6,315 (€8,000) — Lanterne Rouge

£6,315 (€8,000) — Stage win

£15,750 (€20,000) — Most aggressive rider

£15,750 (€20,000) — Best young rider

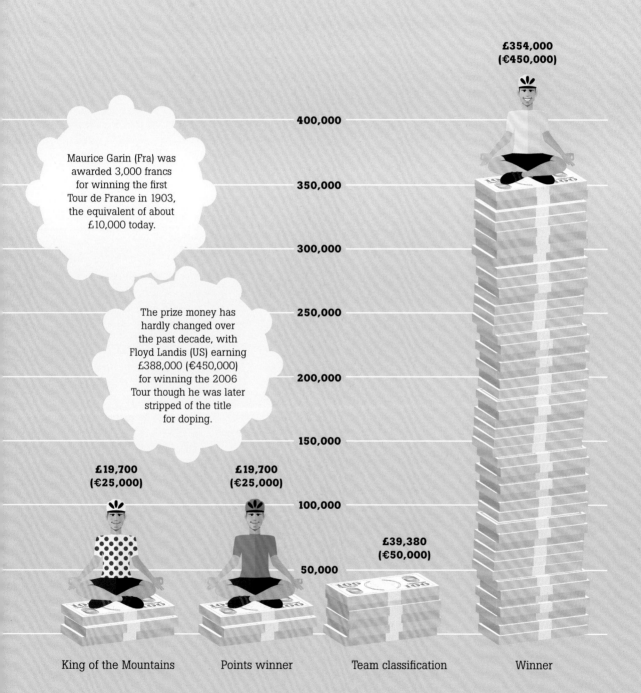

£354,000
(€450,000)

400,000

Maurice Garin (Fra) was
awarded 3,000 francs
for winning the first
Tour de France in 1903,
the equivalent of about
£10,000 today.

350,000

300,000

The prize money has
hardly changed over
the past decade, with
Floyd Landis (US) earning
£388,000 (€450,000)
for winning the 2006
Tour though he was later
stripped of the title
for doping.

250,000

200,000

150,000

£19,700
(€25,000)

£19,700
(€25,000)

£39,380
(€50,000)

100,000

50,000

King of the Mountains

Points winner

Team classification

Winner

The tumultuous history of the 'Women's Tour'

Initially called the Tour Cycliste Féminin and then La Grande Boucle Féminine, the race also known as the 'Women's Tour de France' had a difficult history in the 25 years between its first edition and the last.

1984

Le Tour Cycliste Féminin is held for the first time. It is billed as the 'Women's Tour de France' though the sport's establishment is slow to support it, with the French press questioning whether women will be able to finish the 15-stage, 1,080km race and the reigning Tour champion Laurent Fignon saying he would 'prefer to see women doing something else'.

1989

The brilliant Frenchwoman **Jeannie Longo** wins the event for the third year in a row, having beaten her Italian rival Maria Canins into second place each time. However, the event struggles for sponsorship and does not take place from 1990 until 1992.

1993

The event is reprised with the Dutchwoman **Leontien van Moorsel** winning the first of her two titles. However, it still encounters problems, including having to begin and end stages in cities chosen purely because they contributed funding and regardless of their location. This leads to exhaustingly long transfers between stages.

1998

Société du Tour de France, the organisers of the men's Tour, decide that the women's version has infringed their trademark and force them to change the name of the women's race. It becomes known as **La Grande Boucle Féminine**, meaning The Women's Big Loop.

2004

The Grande Boucle is not held because of lack of sponsorship and what are called 'organisational problems'.

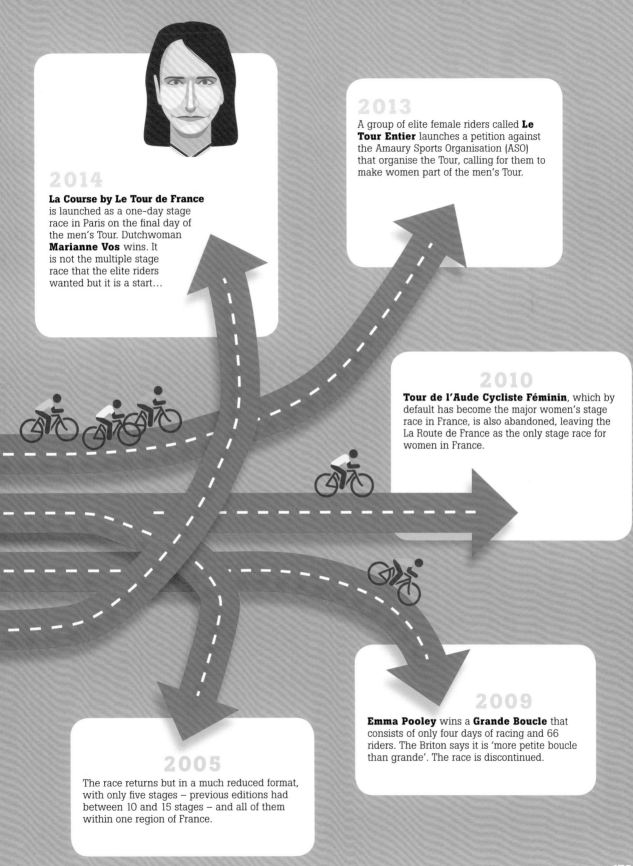

2014

La Course by Le Tour de France is launched as a one-day stage race in Paris on the final day of the men's Tour. Dutchwoman **Marianne Vos** wins. It is not the multiple stage race that the elite riders wanted but it is a start…

2013

A group of elite female riders called **Le Tour Entier** launches a petition against the Amaury Sports Organisation (ASO) that organise the Tour, calling for them to make women part of the men's Tour.

2010

Tour de l'Aude Cycliste Féminin, which by default has become the major women's stage race in France, is also abandoned, leaving the La Route de France as the only stage race for women in France.

2009

Emma Pooley wins a **Grande Boucle** that consists of only four days of racing and 66 riders. The Briton says it is 'more petite boucle than grande'. The race is discontinued.

2005

The race returns but in a much reduced format, with only five stages – previous editions had between 10 and 15 stages – and all of them within one region of France.

Cycling's greatest tragedy

The death of Tom Simpson on Mont Ventoux is arguably the saddest day in the history of the Tour de France and perhaps in the sport itself. Aged only 29 at the time, Simpson, a prolific winner of Classics, the first Briton to wear the Tour's yellow jersey, and his country's first ever winner of the professional World Road Race, was among the most talented and popular road riders of his generation.

July 12 1967

How the disaster unfolded

AFTERNOON

Simpson, the leader of the British team, finishes stage 13 into Marseille in seventh place on the general classification.

EVENING

His agent, Daniel Dousset, puts Simpson under pressure to produce a good result, even though the Brit has been suffering with an upset stomach.

Thomas Simpson

Nickname **Mister Tom**

Birthplace **Haswell, County Durham, England**

Date of birth **November 30, 1937**

Died **July 13, 1967**

July 13
1967

MORNING
The Tour's official doctor, Pierre Dumas, notes the exceptionally hot weather ahead of the Mont Ventoux stage and tells a journalist: 'If the boys stick their nose in a topette today, we could have a death on our hands.' A 'topette' was a bag of drugs.

MID-MORNING
A journalist notices Simpson looking tired at the start line and asks if the temperature is bothering him. 'No, it's not the heat, it's the Tour,' he replies.

MID-AFTERNOON
Simpson slips off the back of an elite group of riders and begins to lose control of his bike, zig-zagging on the road through exhaustion. One kilometre from the summit of Mont Ventoux, he falls off but rejects his team mechanic Harry Hall's suggestion that he should give up and instead gets back in the saddle for another 50 metres before losing consciousness. Lying by the side of the road, he is given mouth-to-mouth resuscitation until Dumas arrives with an oxygen mask.

LATE-AFTERNOON
A police helicopter arrives at the roadside about 40 minutes after Simpson passes out and takes him to Avignon hospital, where he is pronounced dead at 5.40pm. Later, it would be revealed that two empty tubes of amphetamines and a half-full tube of Tonedron, which was a form of methamphetamine, were found in his jersey pocket.

July 14
1967

AFTERNOON
After the British team decides against withdrawing from the Tour, the peloton arranges for one of them to win the 15th stage. The honour falls to Barry Hoban, the sprinter, who some years later was to marry Simpson's widow.

THE AFTERMATH
French authorities attribute Simpson's death to the amphetamines in his system, saying they impaired his judgment and enabled him to push his body beyond its physical limit. His death leads to the introduction of mandatory testing for performance-enhancing drugs. His memorial, paid for by the readers of *Cycling* magazine, is unveiled a year later beside the spot where he collapsed.

'Put me back on my bike'

What were supposedly Simpson's famous last words were actually invented by the journalist Sid Saltmarsh, who was covering the Tour but was not actually present at the scene. Simpson's actual comment, which he directed to Harry Hall, was, 'Me straps, Harry, me straps', as he tried to get his feet back in his toe clips the first time that he fell from his bike.

Cipollini's greatest hits

As one of the most successful sprinters of all time, Mario Cipollini could have been given the 'icon' treatment in this book, but we decided to focus on the Italian pin-up's most memorable outfits instead. Incidentally, cipollini is a type of onion in Italy.

He was fined for wearing an all-yellow kit and using a yellow bike while leading the 1997 Tour de France. The practice, however, became commonplace in later editions of the race.

He wore a Roman tunic during the rest day of the 1999 Tour to celebrate both Julius Caesar's birthday (July 12) and his fourth consecutive stage win, a postwar record.

Cipollini was known for his garish taste in skinsuits and none was more extrovert than the tiger-skin patterned one, although the all-pink number that he wore on the Giro d'Italia prologue came close.

Perhaps his most unusual skinsuit was the 'skinless' one that depicted internal organs. Maybe he was trying to tell the world that there were no dodgy substances going round his system.

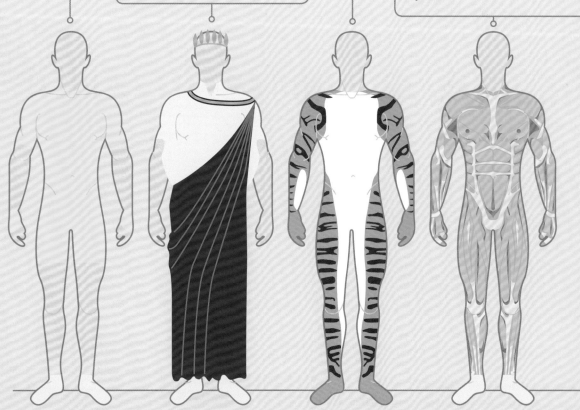

He donned various outfits in adverts for the Italian bike-shoe manufacturer Northwave during his career. Our favourite was the Musketeer gear, though he was also seen in this Batman outfit.

Not the most outlandish of all his kit but unusual nonetheless. This futuristic skinsuit was inspired by *Tron*, the 1982 science-fiction film that combined live action with computer animation.

In 2016, he posted a picture of himself on Facebook wearing nothing but a helmet while training on a turbo. The stunt was in response to criticism of an advert for his bike range in which he rode one without wearing a helmet.

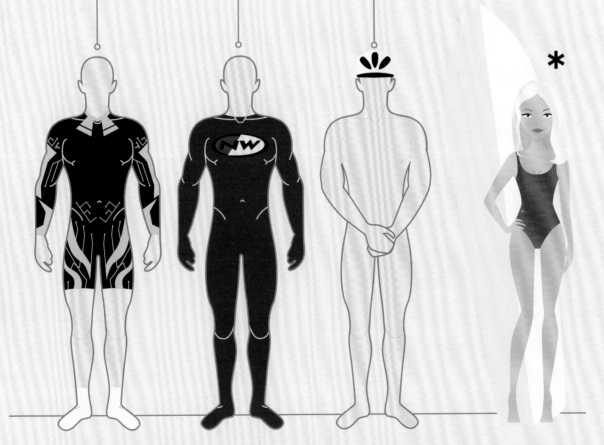

*Cipollini's bike caught the eye too when he taped a picture of the *Baywatch* actress Pamela Anderson to it. Asked why, he said: 'Because I know what my wife looks like.'

The cyclists' network

The Strava website has given cycling fans a great insight into the training and racing regimes of professional riders in recent seasons. By following those members of the peloton who use the site, you can both examine their rides and pit yourself against the pros on the segments of road covered. Here are 10 of the best riders to follow, with statistics that were correct at the time of writing (June 2016).

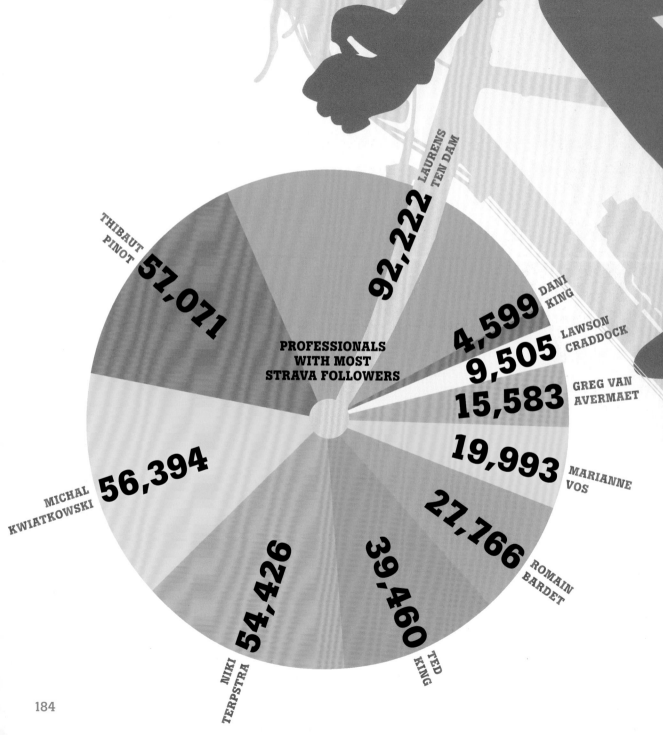

PROFESSIONALS
WITH MOST
STRAVA FOLLOWERS

LAURENS TEN DAM 92,222

THIBAUT PINOT 57,071

DANI KING 4,599

LAWSON CRADDOCK 9,505

GREG VAN AVERMAET 15,583

MARIANNE VOS 19,993

ROMAIN BARDET 27,766

TED KING 39,460

NIKI TERPSTRA 54,426

MICHAL KWIATKOWSKI 56,394

LAURENS TEN DAM
Netherlands
Giant-Alpecin

Ten Dam is among the most popular of all Strava users, thanks to the fact that he uploads just about every ride, both in training and in competition. He also writes blog posts and even sends messages to fans during races, thanking them for supporting him. His average distance per week is a mere 817km.

THIBAUT PINOT
France
FDJ

The brilliant young Frenchman's profile is linked to his Instagram profile so you can follow his travails on the Tour from both a visual and statistical perspective. To his credit, Pinot continued logging his rides on the 2016 Tour even after he fell out of contention for the young rider's jersey.

MICHAL KWIATKOWSKI
Poland
Team Sky

The young Pole delighted Strava users when he uploaded his successful ride to the World Road Race title in 2014. Less prestigious were the relatively modest training rides in his home country that he logged while others on Team Sky were riding to exhaustion on the 2016 Tour.

NIKI TERPSTRA
Netherlands
Etixx-Quick Step

The Dutchman's triumphant ride to the 2014 Paris-Roubaix earnt Terpstra what was then the most ever 'kudos' clicks on Strava, with more than 8,000 users congratulating him on his performance. It also earnt him six Strava 'King of the Mountain' titles for the quickest rides over certain cobbled sectors.

TED KING
USA
retired

King quit racing in 2015 but makes the list because of the important role he played in Strava's growth. One of the first professionals to use it, he set the standard by logging all of his ride data, passing on advice to other users and eventually leading Strava-organised amateur rides.

ROMAIN BARDET
France
AG2R

The winner of the combativity award at the 2015 Tour is another exciting young French rider who is extremely active on Strava. In 2016, he logged nearly all of his competitive rides leading up to the Tour. His peak month was March when he rode for 73 hours, covered 2,800km and climbed almost 40,000m.

MARIANNE VOS
Netherlands
Rabo-Liv Women Cycling Team

The brilliant Dutchwoman's activity on Strava slowed in 2015 as she suffered successive injury problems and then experimented with mountain-biking, but she returned to logging her training rides and races in 2016 as she built up to the Olympic road race, as reigning champion.

GREG VAN AVERMAET
Netherlands
BMC

The Dutchman gave his 2016 Tour rides titles such as 'Another long day in the saddle' – which surely qualifies as an understatement – and 'TdF stage win and yellow', which is not something every Strava user can write. That particular ride earnt the popular Van Avermaet kudos from 429 followers.

LAWSON CRADDOCK
USA
Cannodale-Garmin

The young American rider might consider revealing a little less of his suffering on Strava as his status grows within the peloton. As his debut Tour grew increasingly hard in 2016, he gave his rides titles such as 'Stage eight – wtf happened out there?' which possibly did not go down well with sponsors.

DANI KING
Great Britain
Wiggle-Honda

A world and Olympic champion on the track, King is among the most followed female professionals to use Strava. As it happens, the website actively supports their racing scene, having sponsored the Queen of the Mountains competition at the Women's Tour of Britain, awarding an orange polka-dot jersey based on the Strava branding and the famous Tour equivalent jersey.

ICON Chris Froome

From an unlikely introduction to cycling that involved riding dirt tracks as a child in Kenya, Chris Froome has climbed the ranks of the sport to become the outstanding stage-racer of his generation, winning his third Tour de France title in four years in 2016. Born in Nairobi to British parents, after his early years in mountain biking he learnt his craft on the South African road-racing scene before eventually Team Sky's Dave Brailsford took a gamble on the young Froome, despite him being an awkward, inconsistent if also clearly talented rider. Once he got over a nasty and prolonged bout of the parasitic disease bilharzia while with the British-based team, he scarcely looked back, successfully building his seasons around an assault on the Tour. A phenomenal climber, world-class time-triallist and gentlemanly under pressure, Froome's reign over the modern peloton could last for years yet.

THE FACTS

Full name **Christopher Clive Froome**

Nickname **Froomey**

Date of birth **May 20, 1985**

Birthplace **Nairobi, Kenya**

Height **6ft 1in (1.86m)**

Weight **10st 8lb (67.5kg)**

Discipline **Road**

THE TEAMS

2007
Konica-Minolta

2008-09
Barloworld

2010-
Team Sky

THE PHYSICAL TRANSFORMATION

In 2015, three weeks after winning the Tour de France, Froome underwent physiological tests at the GSK Human Performance Laboratory in London. He had taken a similar examination at the start of his professional career in 2007.

2007
Weight **75.8kg**
Body fat **16.9%**
Peak power output
5.56 watts/kilogrammes
Sustained power (over 20-40min)
420 watts
VO2 max
80.2 mililitres of oxygen/kg/min

2015
Weight **69.9kg - he had put on 3kg since his victory**
Body fat **9.8%**
Peak power output **7.51w/kg**
Sustained power **419W**
VO2 max **85 ml/kg/min**

STAGE-RACE WINS

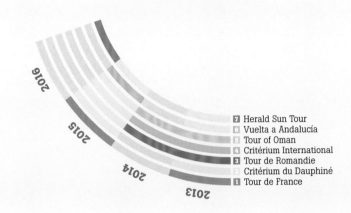

- **7** Herald Sun Tour
- **6** Vuelta a Andalucía
- **5** Tour of Oman
- **4** Critérium International
- **3** Tour de Romandie
- **2** Critérium du Dauphiné
- **1** Tour de France

OTHER ACHEVEMENTS

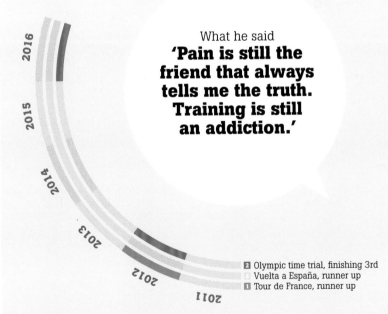

What he said
'Pain is still the friend that always tells me the truth. Training is still an addiction.'

- **3** Olympic time trial, finishing 3rd
- **2** Vuelta a España, runner up
- **1** Tour de France, runner up

Twitterati

Mark Cavendish became the most followed cyclist on Twitter by overtaking Alberto Contador and the straight-talking Manxman has shown no sign of slowing his prodigious output online. As a result, like all the figures here, his will almost certainly have increased by the time you read this.

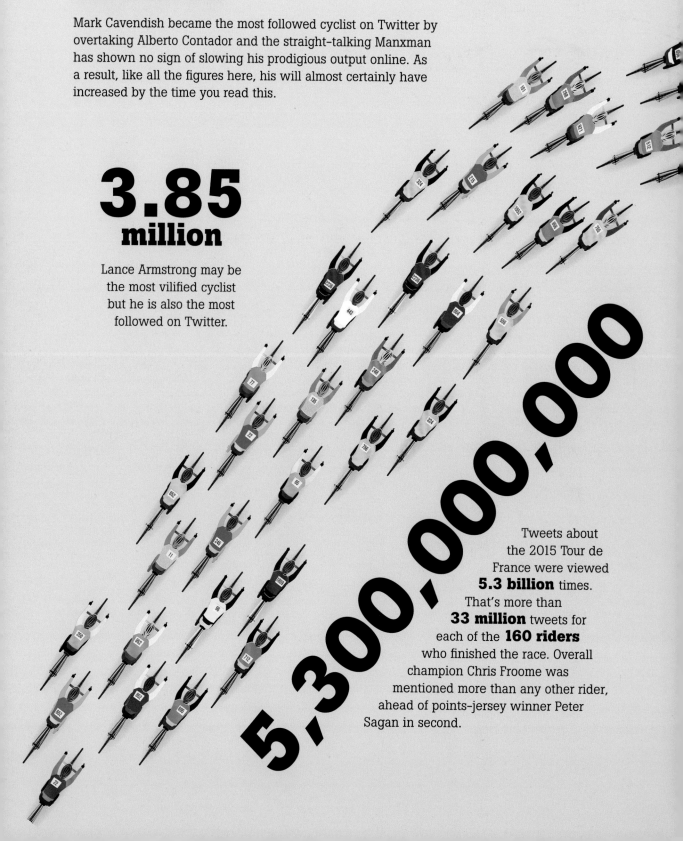

3.85 million

Lance Armstrong may be the most vilified cyclist but he is also the most followed on Twitter.

5,300,000,000

Tweets about the 2015 Tour de France were viewed **5.3 billion** times. That's more than **33 million** tweets for each of the **160 riders** who finished the race. Overall champion Chris Froome was mentioned more than any other rider, ahead of points-jersey winner Peter Sagan in second.

AHEAD OF THE BUNCH

Canadian all-rounder Christian Meier was the first professional cyclist to sign up to Twitter back in March 2008. He waited to make his move, though, sending his first tweet in November 2012.

TEAM CLASSIFICATION

1 Team Sky (612,000 followers)
2 Movistar Team (369k)
3 BMC Racing Team (185k)
4 Etixx Quick-Step (181k)
5 Cannondale Pro Team (160k)
6 Tinkoff-Saxo (138k)
7 ORICA-GreenEDGE (131k)
8 Astana (112k)
9 Team Giant-Alpecin (102k)
10 LottoNL-Jumbo (90k)
11 Lotto Soudal (86k)
12 MTN-Qhubeka (77k)
    = Team Dimension Data (77k)
13 Team Katusha (71k)
14 Team Lampre Merida (61k)
15 AG2R La Mondiale (58k)
16 FDJ (51k)
17 Team COFIDIS (34k)
18 Team IAM Cycling (30k)
19 BORA-ARGON 18 (23k)
20 Team Europcar (11k)
    = Trek Factory Racing (11k)

TWITTER DREAM TEAM

Mark Cavendish	**1.15m** followers
Alberto Contador	**1.09m**
Chris Froome	**920,000**
Nairo Quintana	**539,000**
Fabian Cancellara	**457,000**
Peter Sagan	**412,000**
Vincenzo Nibali	**402,000**
Geraint Thomas	**244,000**
Frank Schleck	**223,000**

The lanterne rouge

The Lanterne Rouge is the tag given to the last-placed competitor in the Tour de France, with the name inspired by the red lantern that once hung on the back of railway trains to illuminate their rear. For years, the position was coveted by also-rans because the Lanterne Rouge earned bigger contracts at the post-Tour criteriums. More recently, riders have coveted the publicity it earns their teams, which has ensured the battle for it has produced some interesting tales…

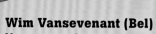

Wim Vansevenant (Bel)

Vansevenant has won the Lanterne Rouge more times than any other rider, finishing last three years in succession between 2006-08, although the Belgian insisted that he had not pursued the position. 'The Lanterne Rouge is not a position you go for,' he said. 'It comes for you.'

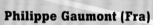

Philippe Gaumont (Fra)

In 1997, the late Gaumont suddenly put on weight in the build-up to the Tour as the result of an experimental drugs regime. Realising that he would have no impact on the race, his Cofidis team management ordered the Frenchman to finish last to gain publicity. He managed it by a full eight minutes, which was helped in part by him faking illness on one of the closing stages.

Tony Hoar (GB)

Hoar earned himself a little fame when he won the Lanterne Rouge in 1955 on a race that was not only his first Tour but also the first time he had actually ridden in mountains. The second Briton ever to finish the Tour behind his team-mate Brian Robinson, Hoar had not meant to come last but given that only 69 of the 120 entrants finished, in truth it was no mean feat.

Gerhard Schönbacher (Aut)

In 1979, Schönbacher kissed the road before the finish in Paris such was his delight at claiming the Lanterne Rouge. The Austrian had fought a close battle for the honour with Philippe Tesnière (Fr), who had been last a year earlier. Especially memorable were their deliberately poor time trials in which both took a laughable 15 minutes more than the stage winner Bernard Hinault.

Jacky Durand (Fra)

In 1999, Durand won both the Lanterne Rouge and the award for the most combative rider. The Frenchman ensured the former honour by deliberately dropping to the back of the field on one of the final stages after a series of solo attacks had come to nothing.

€8,000

In 2015, Tour officials embraced the tradition and introduced a Lanterne Rouge jersey for its last-placed rider, as well as €8,000 (£6,300) prize money, the same as for winning a stage.

'The lanterne rouge is not a position you go for... it comes for you.'

Wim Vansevenant

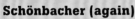

Schönbacher (again)

The Tour organisers believed the attention given to the battle for the Lanterne Rouge demeaned the race and tried to end it in 1980 by eliminating the last rider on the General Classification between the 14th and 20th stages. However, Schönbacher deliberately rode near-last each day and still managed to scoop the 'prize', prompting officials to abandon the rule the following year.

Jimmy Casper (Fra)

Lanterne Rouge in 2001 and 2004, Casper viewed his achievement as a badge of honour because he managed to finish races during the Armstrong era of widespread blood boosting. 'I still have a sense of pride in being able to say that I finished those Tours a l'eau,' the sprinter said, by which he meant he took nothing more incriminating than water. 'It was a kind of courage.'

Quarto is the authority on a wide range of topics.
Quarto educates, entertains and enriches the lives of
our readers – enthusiasts and lovers of hands-on living.

www.QuartoKnows.com

ACKNOWLEDGEMENTS

The information used in this book was taken from a variety of sources both in print and online. Books used included:

Boulting, Ned, *On the road bike: The search for a nation's cycling soul*, Yellow Jersey, London, 2013.

Burton, Beryl and Kirby, Colin, *Personal Best: The autobiography of Beryl Burton*, Mercian Manuals, West Yorkshire, 1986.

Cossins, Robert, *The Monuments: The grit and the glory of Cycling's greatest one-day races*, Bloomsbury, London, 2014.

Dineen, Robert, *Kings of the Road: A journey into the heart of British Cycling*, Aurum Press, London, 2015.

Dineen, Robert, *Reg Harris: The rise and fall of Britain's greatest cyclist*, Ebury Press, London, 2012.

Fallon, Lucy and Adrian Bell, *Viva La Vuelta!: The story of Spain's great bike race*, Mousehold Press, 2005.

Fotheringham, William, *Cyclopedia: It's all about the bike*, Yellow Jersey, London, 2010.

Fotheringham, William, *Fallen Angel: The passion of Fausto Coppi*, Yellow Jersey, London, 2009.

Fotheringham, William, *Merckx: Half Man, Half Bike*, Yellow Jersey, London, 2013.

Fotheringham, William, *Put Me Back On My Bike: In search of Tom Simpson*, Yellow Jersey, London, 2007.

Fotheringham, William, *Roule Britannia: A history of Britons in the Tour de France*, Yellow Jersey, London, 2005.

Hilton, Tim, *One More Kilometre and We're in the Showers: Memoirs of a cyclist*, Harper Perennial, London, 2004.

Howard, Paul, *Sex, Lies and Handlebar Tape: The remarkable life of Jacques Anquetil*, Mainstream, London, 2008.

Leonard, Max, *Lanterne Rouge: The last man in the Tour de France*, Yellow Jersey, London, 2014.

McKay, Feargal, *The Complete Book of the Tour de France*, Aurum Press, London, 2014.

Moore, Richard and Benson, Daniel, *Bike!: A tribute to the world's greatest cycling designers*, Aurum Press, London, 2012.

Moore, Richard, *Étape: The untold story of the Tour de France's defining stages*, HarperSport, London, 2015.

Moore, Richard, *Slaying the Badger: LeMond, Hinault and the greatest ever Tour de France*, Yellow Jersey, London, 2011.

Nicholson, Geoffrey, *The Great Bike Race*, Hachette, London, 1978.

Rendell, Matt; *The Death of Marco Pantani: A biography*, Weidenfeld & Nicholson, London, 2006.

RoadCyclingUK, *Infographic Guide to Cycling*, Bloomsbury, London, 2014.

Sidwells, Chris, *Tour Climbs: The complete guide to every mountain stage on the Tour de France*, Aurum Press, London, 2008.

Sykes, Herbie, *Maglia Rosa: Triumph and tragedy at the Giro d'Italia*, Bloomsbury, London, 2011.

Walsh, David, *The Program: Seven Deadly Sins – My pursuit of Lance Armstrong*, Simon & Schuster, London, 2012.

Magazines and newspapers used included *Cycling Weekly*, *Pro Cycling*, *Cyclist*, *Rouleur*, *The Times*, the *Guardian*, the *Independent* and the *Telegraph*. Information was also sourced from several websites, including Cycling News, cyclingarchives.com, Velo Veritas, as well as those of the BBC and Sky Sports.

A big thank you to Richard Green and Lucy Warburton at Aurum Press for commissioning this book and, in Lucy's case, for expertly managing its production. Roger St Pierre did an excellent job of editing it. Luke Browne contributed valuable research and copy.

Illustrated portraits © Paul Oakley
Various symbols and icons adapted from artworks supplied by The Noun Project (thenounproject.com). All other images adapted from artworks © Shutterstock.com or illustrated by Nick Clark, Jane McKenna and Paul Oakley.

First published in Great Britain 2017 by Aurum Press Ltd
74–77 White Lion Street
Islington
London N1 9PF

Text copyright © Robert Dineen 2017

Robert Dineen has asserted his moral right to be identified as the Author of this Work in accordance with the Copyright Designs and Patents Act 1988.

Every effort has been made to verify the accuracy of data up to the end of August 2016. Some statistics will inevitably change over time, but the publishers will be glad to rectify in future editions any omissions brought in writing to their attention. Some statistics will change quicker than others. Please refer to the credited sources for latest information.

A catalogue record for this book is available from the British Library.

ISBN 978 1 78131 642 9
Ebook ISBN 978 1 78131 683 2

1 3 5 7 9 10 8 6 4 2
2017 2019 2021 2020 2018

Design: www.fogdog.co.uk
Illustrated portraits: Paul Oakley
Infographic illustration: Nick Clark, Jane McKenna, Paul Oakley

Printed in China

FSC
www.fsc.org
MIX
Paper from responsible sources
FSC® C008047